ALIVE IN CHRIST

DAVID A. WOMACK

Radiant BOOKS

Gospel Publishing House/Springfield, Mo. 65802

02-0888

ALIVE IN CHRIST

© 1975 by the Gospel Publishing House, Springfield, Missouri
65802. All rights reserved. Adapted from *How to Live the Christian Life* by R. L. Brandt, © 1963 by the Gospel Publishing House.
Library of Congress Catalog Card No. 75-22609. Printed in the
United States of America.

ISBN 0-88243-888-3

A teacher's guide for group study with this book is available from
the Gospel Publishing House (order no. 32-0162).

Contents

Contents

1 Now You're a Child of God

A young minister graduated from Bible college and became the pastor of a small church. He was quite pleased with his newly acquired education, for he had made up his mind he would not stumble through the English language as his preacher father had done.

You can imagine his surprise when an elderly member of his congregation came up to him after his first sermon and said, "It was so good to hear you. You preach just like your father."

LIKE FATHER, LIKE SON

When you accepted Jesus Christ as your Saviour, you became a child of God. And, like all children, you will begin to take on some of the characteristics of your father.

You really are God's child. It's not just a figure of speech. Jesus taught Nicodemus (see John 3:1-21) that salvation is a personal experience of being born again. He said, "Except a man be born again, he cannot see the kingdom of God" (John 3:3).

You probably have asked the same question that Nicodemus asked Jesus: How can a person be born twice? Jesus replied that there are two births, one of the flesh and another of the Spirit.

A person who has been born only once lives entirely on a material level and is spiritually dead; while the one who has been born again has become spiritually alive. It is through this new birth that you have become a child of God. You have been born into His great family.

Don't think you may someday become a child of God if you are good enough. If you sincerely accepted Jesus Christ as your Saviour and asked Him to forgive your sins, you already have become His child. The apostle John said, "Beloved, now are we the sons of God, and it doth not yet appear what we shall be: but we know that, when he shall appear, we shall be like him; for we shall see him as he is" (1 John 3:2).

Family members usually share some of the same general features, for they inherit some traits and learn others from the common contact in the same household. Jesus was so much like His Father that He could say, "He that hath seen me hath seen the Father" (John 14:9).

When you lived in sin, you were, in the words of the Bible, a child of the devil. But since you have become a child of God you are experiencing many changes in your life. That is why the apostle Paul wrote, "Therefore if any man be in Christ, he is a new creature: old things are passed away; behold, all things are become new" (2 Corinthians 5:17). Of course, you are the same person; but you are changed because you have a new nature—that of God, your Father.

You may be puzzled to find that your reactions to the world and to other people have changed. This delightful discovery is nothing less than the same divine nature that was in Jesus Christ. That is why the Bible says, "He that saith he abideth in him ought himself also so to walk, even as he walked" (1 John 2:6).

The similarity is not an accident. The same nature that was in Christ, the Son of God, also manifests itself in the many sons of God. Ahead of you are growth, development, and Christian maturity. Your Heavenly Father will be very patient, but He will expect you to learn to walk and to grow in His grace.

Yet, there is unpretended, easily recognized similarity. It shines out like a light in the darkness. Before, you were ill at ease in the company of Christian people, but now you relish the fellowship of God's other children. You have become a part of a marvelous spiritual family.

The Test of Righteousness

The Lord offers us a simple test of our divine sonship. Jesus said, "Wherefore by their fruits ye shall know them" (Matthew 7:20).

The Bible adds, "In this the children of God are manifest, and the children of the devil: whosoever doeth not righteousness is not of God, neither he that loveth not his brother" (1 John 3:10).

Righteousness most simply stated is obedience to the commands of God, our Father. It involves refraining from what God has forbidden and doing what He has commanded. "And hereby we do know that we know him, if we keep his commandments" (1 John 2:3).

The direction of our walk is a telltale sign of our relationship to God. If we say we are God's children and then deliberately walk contrary to His will, we are only deceiving ourselves (see John 8:34-44).

This does not mean you will walk perfectly with

7

your first step. No father would think of condemning his child who stumbled and fell while learning to walk. The devil will try to discourage you and tell you that you are not God's child; but God does not cast off His sons who falter through inexperience or weakness. Rather, He has made abundant provision for you to get back on your feet and walk (see 1 John 2:1-6).

LOVE: A FAMILY TRAIT

One of the first things a new Christian notices about the children of God is that they love one another. True Christians are nice to each other and to all the world in general.

This love starts with God himself. "For God so loved the world, that he gave his only begotten Son, that whosoever believeth in him should not perish, but have everlasting life" (John 3:16).

A real Christian loves the Lord, his fellow believers, and the people of the world for whom Jesus died on the cross.

It is not easy to love everybody. Some people naturally attract you, while others seem to antagonize or annoy you. However, if you will remember the pit of sin from which the Lord has saved you, it will help you to have compassion for all other people.

Jesus said, "Thou shalt love thy neighbor as thyself" (Matthew 19:19). The problem is that we do not always like ourselves very much. We say things and do things that make ourselves unhappy and guilty. Then we treat other people badly.

It is not hard to love other people if you will remember what a miracle of grace God has done for you and if you will maintain an attitude of gratefulness. Stop reacting to external happenings and be nice because you are God's child and because of what your Father has done for you. Think what would have happened if Jesus had stopped loving the people who mistreated Him!

LOVING TRIPS TO THE WOODSHED

Some of the words most dreaded by any child are: "This is going to hurt me more than it hurts you." That fearful pronouncement usually comes just before a spanking.

At the time, you probably could discern little parental love in your trips to the woodshed, but you later realized how very important were those times of discipline. A pampered child seldom turns out well.

Correction is a sure sign of sonship. Blessed is the believer who realizes this. Some of God's children become greatly troubled when suffering afflicts them, and they begin to think that trouble is a sign that God does not like them or that they are not God's sons.

You may as well realize it now: One who is a real son will find God continually dealing with him and correcting him. God is interested in more than our present feelings, for He is looking out for our eternal well-being.

The Bible says, "For whom the Lord loveth he chasteneth, and scourgeth every son whom he receiveth" (Hebrews 12:6).

God's purpose in disciplining you is to develop your character. You will not mature in the faith if your faith is not tested. Therefore, the Lord allows you to face adversity and trials for your own good.

The correcting process can take many different forms, depending on the individual's need, temperament, and other characteristics. It is common in an earthly family that one child can be corrected with merely a word, while another will not respond without more severe measures. So it is in God's family. All who are sons will be corrected by one means or another.

The Lord most often corrects us with His Word. "All Scripture is given by inspiration of God, and is profitable for doctrine, for reproof, for correction, for instruction in righteousness: that the man of God may be perfect, thoroughly furnished unto all good works" (2 Timothy 3:16, 17).

Regardless of God's method, the fact remains that when you find yourself being corrected you can take courage that it is an evidence that you are God's child and that He loves you very much.

The Influence of the Spirit

Every true child of God has received of God's Spirit, although he may not yet have been baptized in the Holy Spirit.

John said, "And hereby we know that he abideth in us, by the Spirit which he hath given us" (1 John 3:24). Paul said, "Now if any man have not the Spirit of Christ, he is none of his" (Romans 8:9).

It is often difficult for new converts to understand the difference between the general working of the Holy Spirit in their lives and the specific baptism in the Holy Spirit. The fact is that the Spirit of God leads the new convert to his moment of salvation, and He continues to be with him and to influence him after the new birth.

The baptism in the Holy Spirit is a very important personal experience, which we will study in another chapter. During this special baptism the Lord will fill you with His Spirit and will give you an intense desire and power to become His witness to the unsaved people in your community and in your world.

Yet, the Spirit is very real to the new convert. It is by the Spirit that you have become sensitive to spiritual things and have begun to understand and to enjoy the things of God.

THE WITNESS OF THE SPIRIT

One of the most important activities of the Holy Spirit following the new birth is that "the Spirit itself beareth witness with our spirit, that we are the children of God" (Romans 8:16).

This witness of the Spirit is more easily experienced than defined. It is knowledge of our true Father-son relationship, planted deeply within the inner man. We know we have become the sons of God. This is more than mere doctrinal belief; it is direct, personal knowledge.

Because of its intuitive nature, the witness of the Spirit is not always recognized and understood. Some have thought that until a person experiences certain feelings he is not saved; but this belief results in the pursuit of feelings and ends in frustration. Such an approach may make a person think he is not saved unless he feels saved, and may cause him to place his faith in changeable emotions rather than in the changeless Word of God.

The pursuit of certain feelings is a fruitless occupation. The more you seek to feel saved, the less apt you are to feel saved. Even the mighty reformer Martin Luther had sad experiences along this line.

11

It was only after he had learned the way of the Lord more perfectly that he wrote:

> "For feelings come and feelings go,
> And feelings are deceiving;
> My warrant is the Word of God,
> Naught else is worth believing."

Although you must not be sidetracked into the pursuit of feelings, on the other hand you must learn to recognize the Spirit's witness. Perhaps it may best be regarded as a sense of completeness, of personal unity with the Heavenly Father. Galatians 4:6 puts it in vivid focus: "And because ye are sons, God hath sent forth the Spirit of his Son into your hearts, crying, Abba, Father." In ancient times, a Jewish child addressed his father as "Abba."

The witness of the Spirit, then, is the presence of God's Spirit in your heart. It is what causes your soul fearlessly and unashamedly to call God "Father," much as a child intimately calls his father "Daddy."

The Leading of the Spirit

As a child of God, you now have the tremendous advantage of divine guidance through the complicated maze of life. Paul said, "For as many as are led by the Spirit of God, they are the sons of God" (Romans 8:14).

The Spirit's priority assignment is to lead men to Christ. He speaks, convicts, reveals, and draws; but it is man's own response that determines the outcome.

Secondly, the Spirit will seek to lead the new convert into altering his behavior. Certain things you did before your new birth will now seem repugnant and wrong, while other things you never did before will suddenly appeal to you. The Spirit is leading you to become a very nice person with a high sense of morality and a deep feeling of compassion for other people.

Finally, the Spirit will lead you into service for the Lord. When Jesus was on earth, He was constantly led by the Spirit. The Bible is filled with examples of men who did the will of God because they were directed by the Spirit.

You will begin to experience inclinations to become involved in certain ministries of the church, such as to sing in the choir, participate in Bible study groups, or talk to people about what Christ has done in your life. This is the leading of the Spirit to Christian service.

The Spirit seeks to lead all men, but not all will allow themselves to be led. As a child of God, you will want to yield when the Spirit presses you and to follow when He seeks to lead you.

WITNESS TO THREE WORLDS

When you became a child of God, the inhabitants of three worlds saw the evidence of your transformation. The angels in heaven rejoiced over the event, the members of the household of faith detected a new kinship of spirit, and the ungodly world quickly recognized the change in your life.

Although some of your Godly characteristics may not be apparent immediately, you will increasingly develop divine traits over the years if you continue to mature in the Christian faith.

The question of sonship sometimes plagues a child in an earthly family. A young girl, one of seven children, somehow got the idea that she was not really born into the family. She thought she had been acquired in some other way and that her parents were keeping the facts of her origin hidden from her.

But as she grew older, the signs of true family relationship became increasingly more evident to her. She saw in herself the unmistakable resemblance to her own brothers and sisters. Her doubts vanished, and she knew she was truly a part of the family.

When you accepted Jesus Christ as your Saviour, you were born into the family of God.

2 A Diet for Christian Growth

The famous French writer and food expert Brillat-Savarin said, "Tell me what you eat, and I will tell you what you are." Modern doctors put it even more tersely: "You are what you eat."

True as this principle may be for the development of the physical body, it is doubly important for the growth of spiritual life. Your spirit requires a very special diet of heavenly nutrition, for what you grow to become spiritually will be the real you that will live forever.

As a new convert, you are but a babe in Christ. You must be sure to eat and drink the right spiritual diet so you will grow up big and strong like Christ himself.

A Very Special Milk

The human body needs lots of milk, meat, fruit, and vegetables to grow into adult health and vitality. In much the same way, your spiritual life requires certain nutrients to survive and to develop into full Christian maturity.

As a newly born-again Christian, you share a basic need with all infants. You require milk. And, as always, the Bible has just what you need. Peter said,

"As newborn babes, desire the sincere milk of the word, that ye may grow thereby: if so be ye have tasted that the Lord is gracious" (1 Peter 2:2,3).

These words are so important that we need to take a closer look at them. In his previous chapter, Peter had just talked about "Being born again, not of corruptible seed, but of incorruptible, by the word of God, which liveth and abideth for ever" (1 Peter 1:23). Now, he goes on to say that a newborn babe needs the "milk of the word" so he will grow.

By calling it the "sincere milk of the word," Peter meant that the Word of God is genuine, precisely what you need for spiritual growth. The Word of God is prepared exactly to provide the correct spiritual ingredients for your Christian development.

If you look closely at the passage, you will see that Peter has given you the secret for enjoying your Bible reading. He says you are to desire the Word of God. You are supposed to yearn for Bible reading (and Bible preaching) as a baby desires milk. It would be hard to imagine a stronger hunger than that!

But how do you develop such an appetite for the Bible? That is where the secret comes in. Peter says that when you drink this milk of the Word you actually will taste the goodness of the Lord! When you read the Bible and listen to Bible preaching, you feed on God and His truth. And Peter says you will find out for yourself that the Lord tastes very good. It is an open invitation to come back and feed your soul again and again at this holy table.

The Bible and its preaching are not like other foods, for they cannot be overeaten. The more you read the Word of God and hear its preaching the more healthy will become your spiritual life. Of course, you will not want to neglect your human duties or spend so much time feeding your own spirit that you fail to take Christ to other people. A Christian should be the most normal, well-balanced person in his community.

Unlike other books, the Bible never runs out of new truth. The deeper you go in Bible study, the more you find. No one in the history of the world yet has discovered the bottom of God's marvelous bowl.

As you mature in the faith, you will outgrow your first need for a newborn baby's milk and will find that the Bible offers you a stronger diet of meat. The Bible says, "For every one that useth milk is unskilful in the word of righteousness: for he is a babe. But strong meat belongeth to them that are of full age, even those who by reason of use have their senses exercised to discern both good and evil" (Hebrews 5:13,14).

Throughout your life, the Word of God will provide your whole spiritual diet. If you begin with the genuine milk in your spiritual infancy and gradually develop your appetite for the stronger meat of true Bible study, you will grow into a fully mature Christian.

Some Rules for Your Diet

All diets have at least one thing in common: They are intended to produce some sort of change in the dieter's internal nature. For this reason, it is best to follow a doctor's orders.

The Lord's spiritual diet is no exception. You will benefit much more from it if you know something about it and are willing to follow a few basic rules.

The Bible has the appearance of a book, but it is in reality a whole library. Within the covers of this single volume are 66 books, written by a large number of different authors representing periods of time extending over thousands of years and yet all inspired by God to represent His Word to men. It is divided into two parts, the Old and New Testaments. The Old Testament is made up of the Jewish Scriptures, all of which were written before the time of Christ. The New Testament is made up of the Christian Scriptures, written after the time of Christ.

Rule 1: Read the Bible every day. Set up a regular time for your daily Bible reading and follow your plan faithfully. If you read three chapters each day Monday through Saturday and five chapters on Sunday, you will read the whole Bible in one year.

Rule 2: Don't begin on the first page. Start with the four Gospels at the beginning of the New Testament, and then proceed to the Acts, Epistles, and Revelation. After that, you may read the Old Testament.

Rule 3: Interpret the Bible literally, unless the passage is obviously figurative. Remember that the first five books of the New Testament are the story of Jesus and the development of the first churches. The rest of the New Testament is made up of letters written by the apostles. Much of the Old Testament is ancient history, some of it is poetry, and some is prophecy concerning the destiny of early nations. Keep watching for passages that foretold the coming of Christ and His future kingdom.

Rule 4: Read the Bible devotionally. As you read it, look for ways that its words may apply to your life. Ask the Lord to reveal His Word to you, for the same Holy Spirit who inspired its writing can inspire your reading.

Rule 5: Read the Bible studiously. If some topic captures your interest, look up other passages on the same subject. Get a good Bible with a concordance in the back and learn how to look up subjects by searching for key words. You may enjoy reading one of the paraphrased Bibles now available, but you can't trust such loose translations for exact meanings. You should own a King James Version of the Bible and use it for your basic Bible reading.

Rule 6: Carry your Bible to church. Open it to the passage from which the minister is preaching or teaching. You will get much more out of church in this way.

Rule 7: Mark the Bible verses that especially interest or inspire you. It is not sacrilegious to mark the Bible if you are doing it to enhance your benefit from the Word. Most inks show through Bible paper, so you will do best to use a colored pencil or India ink.

As you grow in the knowledge of the Scriptures, your faith will grow. Paul said, "So then faith cometh by hearing, and hearing by the word of God" (Romans 10:17). Do not control your appetite for the Word, but "Let the word of Christ dwell in you richly" (Colossians 3:16).

You Can Talk With Your Father

Yes, your spiritual diet is important to your development. But there is more. You also will learn a new kind of conversation; for you must learn to talk with God.

Prayer is a two-way conversation. You talk to God and you listen; God listens to you, and He talks. Open communication with heaven is a major proof

19

of the truth of the Christian religion. God really hears you and answers.

One of the most marvelous promises in the Bible is found in 1 John 5:14,15: "And this is the confidence that we have in him, that, if we ask any thing according to his will, he heareth us: and if we know that he hear us, whatsoever we ask, we know that we have the petitions that we desired of him."

Real prayer is based on acquaintance with God. John said that to receive answers to our prayers we must know that He hears us. Once you know God personally and have established a speaking and listening relationship with Him, you know He hears you and you can believe without restraint. Doubtless faith is the key to answered prayer.

Apparently, there are no limitations to the potentials of prayer. The only qualifications are an open communication with God, a belief that He hears you, and the faith that He will answer.

To be effective prayer must come from the heart. For this reason, neither formal prayer nor the repetition of memorized lines often qualifies as Biblical prayer. When Jesus taught His disciples to pray, He said, "After this manner therefore pray ye" (Matthew 6:9). The Lord's Prayer is beautiful, especially when Christians say it in unison; but it was intended originally as a pattern for spontaneous prayer.

There are many aspects to prayer, for communication with God is as varied as the people who engage in it. No two prayers are exactly alike, because no two people are alike.

Generally, prayer should begin with reverence and worship. It should be addressed to God. That is why Jesus began with "Our Father which art in heaven." However, we pray in the name of Jesus; for it is our

Lord Jesus Christ who gives us the authority to approach the throne of God. He said, "And whatsoever ye shall ask in my name, that will I do, that the Father may be glorified in the Son" (John 14:13).

Don't forget to thank the Lord for what He has done for you and is doing right now. A thankful child is much more apt to receive good things from his parents than an unthankful one.

As beautiful as some prayers may be, some of the most effective ones are short and to the point. A sudden cry of the name of Jesus in a moment of emergency will bring an immediate response from heaven.

There is a deep experience in prayer that goes beyond the communication of words. That is why the Bible speaks of prayer and supplication. You will want to gather with other Christians at a church altar or prayer meeting and pour out your heart to God. Don't be afraid to let yourself weep or to raise your hands in longing toward your Heavenly Father. Don't be concerned if normal words do not come; you may be praying from the very depths of your being where language cannot express what you want to say.

For further instructions on prayer, read what Jesus said about it in Matthew 6:5-15. Prayer is the key that opens the gates of heaven and ushers you into the very presence of God.

TELL THE WHOLE WORLD!

One of the first reactions of a new Christian is that he wants to tell everybody about his wonderful discovery. The proclamation of the gospel is an important part of the Christian experience, for Jesus said, "Go ye into all the world, and preach the gospel to every creature" (Mark 16:15).

You have to talk to other people about Jesus Christ; for it is part of your nature now that you are a child of God. Your testimony will put fiber in your soul. You will commit yourself publicly and identify yourself with Christ and His church.

The heart and the mouth are closely allied in the healthy Christian's experience. With the heart we believe, and with the mouth we confess (see Romans 10:9,10). Jesus said, "For out of the abundance of the heart the mouth speaketh" (Matthew 12:34).

A Scottish preacher named W. W. Gauld said, "There is no poverty so dire and so humiliating as the spiritual poverty that has nothing to give to the hungry hearts of men. There is no shame like the shame of man or woman who claims to be a Christian and dares not speak the name of Christ" (*The Almoners of God*).

Bold testimony is also a way of opposing the devil. "And they overcame him by the blood of the Lamb, and by the word of their testimony; and they loved not their lives unto the death" (Revelation 12:11). God reached us by His Word, and it is by our words that we continue to spread the gospel and push back the powers of evil.

It is a psychological fact that the person who gives expression to a conviction, by that very act strengthens the conviction. Let a conviction go unexpressed and it soon will pale into insignificance. Every testimony given is like another stake driven to hold a tent steady in a storm.

Some Christians have the mistaken idea that they don't have to talk about Jesus Christ, but can get by with only living the life before their friends. The fact is that a silent Christian is not living the life! The glow and glory of your experience in Christ will fade if you do not give it expression in direct testimony. It is the command of Christ.

ONE PLUS ONE EQUALS THREE!

When two or more Christians meet together in the name of Jesus, a strange and wonderful thing happens; they become the church in action. Jesus said, "For where two or three are gathered together in my name, there am I in the midst of them" (Matthew 18:20).

Jesus has promised to be with all believers, but when two or more Christians gather in His name they become something more than the sum of their individual personalities and experiences. Together, they become the body of Christ in worship and work; for the smallest unit of the church is two people plus Christ.

Because of this miracle, it is very important that every Christian unite himself with a Christ-loving, Bible-believing congregation of believers.

Since you have become a Christian, you probably have noticed how you long to be in worship with other believers. Church attendance is not just a social institution that somehow developed in Western cultures. It is an essential characteristic of Christian people anywhere in the world.

You should join a church and enter fully into its active life. You need the opportunity to worship God in His church, to fellowship with other believers, and to learn more of God's Word. Furthermore, you need the prayer support of other Christians. Make up your mind from the beginning that you will attend church every Sunday and at all other times that you are able.

Worship, evangelistic, and prayer services are very important. But you need more. You need to attend classes in the Bible and in Christian doctrine. Sunday school is for adults, as well as for children, because it offers a full program of religious education. Perhaps before long you will become a Sunday school teacher and help train children, youths, or adults. Try not to miss a single Sunday school class.

Christians are naturally gregarious. For this reason you must take care in your choice of friends. Solomon said, "He that walketh with wise men shall be wise: but a companion of fools shall be destroyed" (Proverbs 13:20).

Join with church friends in fellowship at the house of God; but also get together socially with Christians and talk about spiritual matters. The Bible says, "Not forsaking the assembling of ourselves together, as the manner of some is; but exhorting one another: and so much the more, as ye see the day approaching" (Hebrews 10:25).

A newspaper cartoonist portrayed Abraham Lincoln's humble cabin at the base of a high cliff. On the top of the cliff stood the White House, and extending from the cabin to the White House was a ladder. The caption simply stated, "The ladder is still there."

There is no easy way to attain spiritual maturity, but the ladder is still there for anyone who dares to climb it.

3 The Devil on Parade

If Satan and all his demonic spirits were to march down Broadway while the archangel Michael and the angelic hosts of heaven marched along Strait Street, there is little doubt which parade would attract the largest crowd of spectators.

For some perverse reason buried deeply in his subconscious mind, man always has been fascinated by evil. In most cases, a person does not intend to be wicked or to commit evil acts, but he plays with temptation and flirts with his own spiritual death. As a result of this perversity and curiosity, all men become sinners, and comparatively few ever attain personal salvation.

Jesus said, "For wide is the gate, and broad is the way, that leadeth to destruction, and many there be which go in thereat: because strait is the gate, and narrow is the way, which leadeth unto life, and few there be that find it" (Matthew 7:13,14).

The devil does not want you to walk the strait and narrow way; he wants you with the crowd on Broadway. And he will do everything in his power to lure you from your Christian experience and make you fall into sin. You might just as well learn from the start that you have an enemy who already is at work to destroy you.

The Bible gives you a very simple defense against the devil. It says, "Submit yourselves therefore to God. Resist the devil, and he will flee from you. Draw nigh to God, and he will draw nigh to you" (James 4:7,8). Two words sum it up. Just say "no" to the devil and "yes" to God.

THE ANATOMY OF TEMPTATION

As long as Satan attempts to get you to do things you really don't want to do anyway, you probably will experience little difficulty. It is when your own desires are aroused that you are most apt to sin. This means that the devil cannot make you sin; you only sin when you cooperate in the act.

It is not a sin to be tempted. Even Jesus was tempted, but He was sinless because he resisted the temptation and did not commit sinful acts (sins of commission) or fail to do the necessary acts of righteousness (sins of omission). Jesus "was in all points tempted like as we are, yet without sin" (Hebrews 4:15).

Temptation unresisted leads to sin and tragedy. The starting point is temptation, and the final fruit is death. "Let no man say when he is tempted, I am tempted of God: for God cannot be tempted with evil, neither tempteth he any man: but every man is tempted, when he is drawn away of his own lust, and enticed. Then when lust hath conceived, it bringeth forth sin; and sin, when it is finished, bringeth forth death" (James 1:13-15).

So, you see, your temptation is really your own. Every individual fights his own personal battle with himself and with the devil who seeks to take advantage of his weaknesses.

Yet you cannot fight this battle alone. God has said, "The soul that sinneth, it shall die" (Ezekiel 18:20). That is why Jesus Christ came to the world and died and rose again for your sins. He knew you could not make it alone. He has taken your blame and forgiven your sins. Now live for Him and ask Him to help you overcome the devil and your own personal weaknesses.

ADAM, EVE, AND JESUS

There are three main areas of human temptation: (1) the lust of the flesh, (2) the lust of the eyes, and (3) the pride of life (see 1 John 2:16).

Adam and Eve were tempted in all three. "And when the woman saw that the tree was good for food [the lust of the flesh], and that it was pleasant to the eyes [the lust of the eyes], and a tree to be desired to make one wise [the pride of life], she took of the fruit thereof, and did eat, and gave also unto her husband with her; and he did eat" (Genesis 3:6).

Christ himself was tempted in the same three ways. "Then was Jesus led up of the Spirit into the wilderness to be tempted of the devil" (Matthew 4:1). Satan first tempted Him to turn stones into bread (the lust of the flesh), typifying all temptations to unnatural or immoral satisfaction of physical or sensual appetites.

The next temptation was to throw himself down from a pinnacle of the temple to show the world how God would deliver Him right before the eyes of the people (the lust of the eyes), typifying all temptations to show off before others or to be a willing spectator to a sinful act.

Finally, the devil tempted Christ by offering Him all the kingdoms of the world if He would fall down and worship him (the pride of life), thus typifying the temptations of the human ego.

It also is important to see what the devil hoped to gain from each of these temptations of Christ. In the first, he tried to get the Lord to break His 40-day fast short of serious confrontation with evil. The devil did not ask for the wilderness meeting; it was the Spirit who led Christ to challenge Satan. The devil would rather keep you in a state of noncommitment than allow you to challenge him in the name of Jesus.

In the second temptation Satan hoped to get Christ to put on a spectacular show of His miraculous powers rather than make a serious attack on the world's sicknesses and sins. The devil also will ask you to become a church-hopper and follow the crowds rather than settle down into meaningful ministry to the problems of men.

In the third temptation, the devil tried to get Christ to sell His soul in exchange for worldly power. The Bible asks the question, "For what is a man profited, if he shall gain the whole world, and lose his own soul? or, what shall a man give in exchange for his soul?" (Matthew 16:26). You can be sure the devil will make you a tempting offer. He believes that every man has a price. For some he offers wealth; others are more susceptible to power; and still others will sell out for pleasure. Ultimately, the result is that the person who sells his soul worships Satan.

Eve was an easy victim of temptation, but the Lord Jesus was a strong victor over temptation. Both were tempted in all three points common to man; yet, one was totally defeated while the other was wholly triumphant. Why? The difference was in their response.

Eve reasoned with the serpent; Jesus resisted him. Eve believed the serpent's lie; Jesus rebuked the liar. Eve doubted God's Word; Jesus quoted God's Word.

Knowing you can overcome temptation is half the battle. Paul said, "God is faithful, who will not suffer you to be tempted above that ye are able; but will with the temptation also make a way to escape, that ye may be able to bear it" (1 Corinthians 10:13).

He not only has promised to control your degree of temptation and provide a way to escape; He has offered His own personal help. "For in that he himself hath suffered being tempted, he is able to succor them that are tempted" (Hebrews 2:18).

DRESSED FOR BATTLE

Many people like to talk about the peace of the Christian faith. It is true that Christ brings peace to our inner conflicts; but He does not allow us to live peaceful lives of ease. Rather, He said, "Think not that I am come to send peace on earth: I came not to send peace, but a sword" (Matthew 10:34). He went on to say, "And he that taketh not his cross, and followeth after me, is not worthy of me" (v. 38).

We may experience a wonderful peace in our hearts, but we are engaged in a lifelong battle against the devil and all his evil kingdom.

The Lord has not left us defenseless, but has provided us with all we need to gain the victory. In some ways our armor is like that of a Roman soldier. "Put on the whole armor of God, that ye may be able to stand against the wiles of the devil. For we wrestle not against flesh and blood, but against principalities, against powers, against the rules of the darkness of this world, against spiritual wickedness in high places" (Ephesians 6:11,12).

The Christian's armor is well defined. "Stand therefore, having your loins girt about with truth, and having on the breastplate of righteousness: and your feet shod with the preparation of the gospel of peace; above all, taking the shield of faith, wherewith ye shall be able to quench all the fiery darts of the wicked. And take the helmet of salvation, and the sword of the Spirit, which is the word of God" (vv. 14-17).

Every part of our armor is important. *Truth* heads the list, for there is no greater defense against a lie. *Righteousness* is the chief defense against unrighteousness, for a Christian whose mind is occupied with good thoughts has no time for doing evil. The *gospel of peace* keeps the feet from slipping even when the climb is steep and protects from injury when the pathway is obstructed with snares and pitfalls.

Faith is the Christian's impenetrable shield, for no attack of the devil can overcome it. The head needs protection from temptation, for our heads direct the whole body. *Salvation* is the helmet of this marvelous armor.

The Christian needs only one weapon, the sword of the Spirit, which is the *Word of God*. This was the Saviour's only weapon, and it is all you need to defeat the devil.

Victory over Evil Spirits

The longer you serve Christ the more you will realize that the child of God lives in two worlds—that of matter and that of spirit. When you became spiritually alive, you began to live in that invisible world of spirit where a great conflict is in progress between the forces of heaven and the legions of hell. We do not understand it very well, but we do know that we become deeply involved in the struggle as soon as we become Christians.

In that shadowy world beyond your physical senses there are angels who watch over you and carry out the duties God assigns to them. Also, there are evil spirits associated with the devil. The Bible has much to say about these evil spirits, but there is very little you can know about them that will help you.

You must remember that Satan is a master deceiver. He will do anything to keep your mind off God or the task God has given you. If he can get you to spend your time fighting evil spirits instead of doing more constructive work, he will most certainly do so.

It is harmful to attribute many happenings to evil spirits, even though they may be involved. There is an old saying, "Speak of the devil, and he will appear." If you start trying to identify sicknesses and occurrences with specific demons, you will soon find yourself entangled in a confusing mass of deception.

There are two basic rules for dealing with this dilemma: (1) Treat every manifestation of evil spirits as though it were the devil himself, and (2) don't carry on a conversation with the devil except to cast him from your presence in the name of Jesus Christ of Nazareth.

If you suspect someone is possessed by an evil spirit, do not tell that person what you are thinking; for he may be mentally ill and will attempt to fulfill your expectations, perhaps only for the attention it will bring him. There is such a thing as demon possession, but you should not try to cast out devils alone. In every suspected case, seek the advice of your pastor and the company of other Christians.

It is impossible for an evil spirit to dwell in a true Christian, for Christ will not remain in the same vessel with the devil. When Christ dwells within you, you have absolutely nothing to fear from evil spirits. "Resist the devil, and he will flee from you" (James 4:7).

It is not possible to separate the work of demons from that of the devil himself. Demons are destructive, they employ evil suggestions, and they will deny the Lordship of Jesus Christ. They will not admit that Jesus Christ came in the flesh (see 1 Corinthians 12:3).

The apostle John gave us very good advice: "Beloved, believe not every spirit, but try the spirits whether they are of God . . . Ye are of God, little children, and have overcome them: because greater is he that is in you, than he that is in the world" (1 John 4:1,4).

FALSE DOCTRINE: THE DEVIL'S TRAP

If the devil cannot seduce you with his temptations or deceive you with his evil spirits, he still has another effective device. He will attempt to ensnare you in false teachings.

Paul said, "Now the Spirit speaketh expressly, that in the latter times some shall depart from the faith, giving heed to seducing spirits, and doctrines of devils" (1 Timothy 4:1).

False teaching is a very subtle thing, since it is usually sugarcoated with a thin covering of truth. Therein lies the danger, for in your eagerness to learn you can easily be led astray.

There are several safeguards against false teaching. The greatest is the knowledge of the truth, gained principally from the reading of the Bible and the instruction of Godly men. Insist that every doctrine be proved by the Word of God.

Another safeguard is the counsel and advice of spiritual leaders. "For by wise counsel thou shalt make thy war: and in multitude of counselors there is safety" (Proverbs 25:6). An unteachable spirit is a one-way ticket to error, but a teachable spirit is excellent insurance against it.

Yet another good rule is to know your teacher. "But evil men and seducers shall wax worse and worse, deceiving, and being deceived. But continue thou in the things which thou hast learned and hast been assured of, knowing of whom thou hast learned them" (2 Timothy 3:13,14).

The Holy Spirit will keep you from error, if you will let Him, and "will guide you into all truth" (John 16:13).

IGNORE THE DEVIL

Now that you know about the devil and his crafty ways, put him out of your mind and don't give him another thought. There are three things that make the devil burn with rage: (1) he is powerless when confronted with the name of Jesus Christ and all that His name implies; (2) he cannot break through the resistance of Godly people; and (3) he cannot stand to be ignored.

Jesus had the perfect retort to the devil—"Get thee behind me, Satan: thou art an offense unto me" (Matthew 16:23).

If you want to live a victorious Christian life, don't

listen to the devil, for he has nothing to say that should be of interest to you. Just resist him in the name of Jesus and go on about your Heavenly Father's business.

4 The ABC's of Obedience

In one baptismal service in Colombia a missionary baptized an ex-convict accused of murder, a converted guerrilla fighter, an old woman who had not heard the gospel for the first time until she was 70 years old, a former altar boy, and several young people who had been raised in Assemblies of God families.

No matter what may be in the past, all who come to Jesus Christ for personal forgiveness and salvation must pass through the same waters of baptism and regularly receive the Lord's Supper.

OBEY THE VOICE OF THE LORD

Of all the lessons you must learn as a Christian none is more important than obedience to God. You may learn to sacrifice freely, and that is commendable. You may offer yourself and your means, and that is good. But there is no substitute for obedience.

In Old Testament times, some people thought they had fulfilled their whole obligation to God when they sacrificed an animal as a burnt offering: but the Word of the Lord said, "Hath the Lord as great delight in burnt offerings and sacrifices, as in obeying the voice of the Lord? Behold, to obey is better than sacrifice, and to hearken than the fat of rams" (1 Samuel 15:22).

At the heart of the Great Commission is the command, "Teaching them to observe all things whatsoever I have commanded you" (Matthew 28:20). Obedience must be taught, for until it is learned, spiritual progress will be very limited.

The desire to obey is innate in every Christian; yet it definitely needs direction. A child may be perfectly willing to obey, but until he is taught the required steps of obedience, his fulfillment of his parents' will cannot be complete.

Obedience is a broad term that includes every area of Christian experience. However, there are two acts that must be considered as the ABC's of obedience—water baptism and the Lord's Supper.

Water baptism is a once-in-a-lifetime act, while the Lord's Supper, or the Communion, is to be repeated often. Neither of these ordinances offers merit for salvation, but both have real value and are necessary to fulfill all righteousness.

The Assemblies of God theologian Myer Pearlman wrote:

New Testament Christianity is not a ritualistic religion; at the heart of it is man's direct contact with God through the Spirit. Therefore it does not lay down a hard and fast order of worship but leaves the church in every age and land to adapt the method best suited for the expression of its life. There are, however, two ceremonies which are essential because divinely ordained, namely, water baptism and the Lord's Supper. Because of their sacred character they are sometimes described as sacraments—literally, "sacred things" or "oaths consecrated by a sacred rite"; they are also referred to as ordinances because they are ceremonies "ordained" by the Lord himself.

Water baptism is the rite of entrance into the Christian church, and symbolizes spiritual life begun; the Lord's Supper is the rite of communion and signifies spiritual life continued. The first pictures faith in Christ, the second pictures fellowship with Christ. The first is administered only once, for there can be but one beginning of the spiritual life; the second is administered frequently, teaching that spiritual life must be nourished" (*Knowing the Doctrines of the Bible*, Gospel Publishing House, Springfield, Missouri: 1937, pp. 352-3).

It may be argued that one may be a Christian without participating in water baptism or the Lord's Supper, for the thief on the cross did not do so. God is merciful to those who accept Christ at the time of their death or who for some extraordinary but valid reason cannot be baptized or receive Communion. However, for all who do have the opportunity, the words of Jesus must apply, "If ye love me, keep my commandments" (John 14:15).

The Reason for Baptism

Have you noticed that obedience is always preceded by a commandment? Until a commandment is clearly expressed, it is very unlikely that it will be kept.

The New Testament contains a number of commands related to water baptism. These fall into two categories: (1) commandments given to those who were already disciples to baptize, and (2) commandments given to those who were becoming disciples to be baptized.

The spiritual leadership of the church is under orders to teach, make disciples, and baptize those who believe.

Lest anyone mistakenly believe he does not need to be baptized in water, he should remember that

Christ himself was baptized in the Jordan River for His own need as well as to provide a permanent example to all who would follow in the Christian faith.

The fact that water baptism was ordained by the Lord himself is an indication of its purposefulness. This purpose is threefold: (1) identification, (2) illustration, and (3) initiation.

In the act of baptism you outwardly identify yourself with Christ. You show your union with Christ in death to sin, in burial of your old nature, and in resurrection to newness of life (see Romans 6:4-6). While your actual identification is by faith, your practical demonstration is by water baptism.

Water baptism also is an illustration to you of that which has taken place within you, and it is thus a means of establishing you in your new experience. The watery grave illustrates your death to sin. Immersion in the water speaks of the burial of the old life of sin, and your coming forth out of the water illustrates your resurrection to a new life of righteousness.

From another point of view, water baptism is a sort of initiation ceremony. In a sense, it finalizes your entry into the household of faith.

The primary purpose for water baptism is what it does for the individual being baptized. Nevertheless, baptism also serves a further purpose—that of forceful testimony to others of the grace of God.

The Example of the Early Church

The Assemblies of God places great emphasis on the example of the first-century, Apostolic Church. The church believes in a full return to the doctrines, the religious experiences, the practices, and the priorities of the Apostolic Church.

The Early Church attached much importance to water baptism, and in so doing set a precedent for the church of all ages. In complete obedience to the Great Commission, all new converts were instructed and baptized. This was true of the very first converts after the outpouring of the Holy Spirit on the Day of Pentecost, for "Then Peter said unto them, Repent, and be baptized every one of you in the name of Jesus Christ for the remission of sins, and ye shall receive the gift of the Holy Ghost. . . . Then they that gladly received his word were baptized" (Acts 2:38,41).

Philip followed the same rule in Samaria. "But when they believed Philip preaching the things concerning the kingdom of God, and the name of Jesus Christ, they were baptized, both men and women" (Acts 8:12).

The Ethiopian eunuch, converted on the road to Gaza, evidently learned from the beginning that baptism was an essential element in his obedience to God, for his first inquiry after Philip had preached Jesus to him was, "See, here is water; what doth hinder me to be baptized?" (Acts 8:36).

Paul's experience was similar. "And immediately there fell from his eyes as it had been scales: and he received sight forthwith, and arose, and was baptized" (Acts 9:18). Other early examples may be found in Acts 10:46-48; 16:32,33; and 19:4,5.

THE CORRECT WAY TO BAPTIZE

Because of the importance of baptism, our church insists that the ceremony be done exactly as it was described in the New Testament.

First, the only acceptable formula for baptism is that found in the Great Commission—"Go ye therefore, and teach [make disciples of] all nations, baptizing them in the name of the Father, and of the Son, and of the Holy Ghost" (Matthew 28:19).

The minister baptizing you will say, "I baptize you in the name of the Father, and of the Son, and of the Holy Ghost."

Some people are troubled by Peter's command, "Be baptized every one of you in the name of Jesus Christ" (Acts 2:38). There is no real contradiction. Jesus' command had to do with formula, and the command of Peter had to do with authority. In the *Didache*, a Christian document written about A.D. 100, baptism is described as being in the name of the Lord Jesus, but when the book goes into detail about the rite it prescribes the Trinitarian formula.

The second condition upon which our church insists is that baptism is to be by immersion. That is, the person being baptized is to be immersed completely beneath the water as a representation of burial to the old life and a resurrection to the new.

When Jesus was baptized, He "went up straightway out of the water" (Matthew 3:16). He could not have come up out of the water if He had not been immersed in it. Also, when Philip baptized the Ethiopian, "they went down both into the water" (Acts 8:38).

The practice of sprinkling or pouring water was a later change in the original baptismal rite. Although such methods may be more convenient than immersion, they are nowhere taught in Scripture and are inadequate representations of Christian death and resurrection.

Yet a third point upon which our church insists is that only true believers may be baptized. Baptism is an outward witness to an inward change. For this reason, we do not baptize infants; but only baptize adults and fully knowledgeable youths. (We dedicate babies and their parents to the Lord, somewhat as the Baby Jesus was presented in the temple.)

We feel so strongly about our return to the Biblical form of baptism that we do not accept previous baptism if it was not by immersion and in the name of the Father, Son, and Holy Ghost. If you have become a Christian believer, you need to be baptized soon in the full apostolic manner.

The Lord's Supper

The Lord Jesus gave us very few religious ceremonies. Even with such an important matter as the order for a church service, he did not go into any detailed description. For this reason, we must place great importance on the two ordinances that He did describe—water baptism and the Communion.

There are three names used for the partaking of the bread and wine—the Lord's Supper, the Communion, and the Eucharist. In our church, we tend to use the first two forms because the latter one is often associated with medieval practices.

As with baptism, the Communion is intended only for genuinely converted believers. The ritual partaking of bread and wine (unleavened bread and fresh grape juice) is to remind you of the broken body and shed blood of Jesus Christ, gives you an effective opportunity to seek the present grace of God in your life, and allows you to carry out an act of faith in your future life with Christ in heaven.

41

The elements of the Communion do not in themselves save the soul, but they help you to keep the atonement of Christ fresh in your memory. As such, they become a sort of food for the soul, for they nourish the soul with fresh remembrances of the cross of Christ and all it implies.

The central focus of the Communion is not upon the symbolic bread and wine or even upon the real blood and body, but upon the Lord Jesus Christ himself. The Bible says, "This do ye, as oft as ye drink it, in remembrance of me. For as often as ye eat this bread, and drink this cup, ye do show the Lord's death till he come" (1 Corinthians 11:25,26).

The bread symbolizes the broken body of our Lord. "The Lord Jesus . . . took bread . . . and said, Take, eat: this is my body" (1 Corinthians 11:23,24).

The wine speaks of the Saviour's shed blood. "After the same manner also he took the cup, when he had supped, saying, This cup is the new testament in my blood" (1 Corinthians 11:25).

The Communion is for all God's children. While some churches practice closed Communion, thus limiting the partaking to their own members, the Assemblies of God (in the United States) practices open Communion. Any Christian present may partake. It is his duty to do so, for the Lord commanded, "This do."

CAUTION: IT MAY BE DANGEROUS

Even though all Christians are welcome to partake of the Communion in our services, we must warn that while the Communion service is intended to bless and enrich the church, it can be abused to the damnation of the participant.

In 1 Corinthians 11, the apostle Paul enumerated

three evil consequences that can befall those who partake of the Communion unworthily: (1) "guilty of the body and blood of the Lord" (v. 27), (2) "eateth and drinketh damnation to himself" (v. 29), and (3) "for this cause many are weak and sickly among you, and many sleep" (v. 30).

What can make you unworthy to partake? The answer is plainly stated: "not discerning the Lord's body" (v. 29). Paul referred to the body and blood of the Lord, so we know he was speaking of the physical body of Christ; but it also seems probable that by "the Lord's body" he meant the mystical Body, which is the Church.

In this light, the sin of not discerning the Lord's body is more than a failure to comprehend Christ's passion on the cross; it is a failure by members of the Body to maintain proper relationships with each other.

You may avoid this danger by self-examination. Paul said, "But let a man examine himself, and so let him eat of that bread, and drink of that cup" (1 Corinthians 11:28). Every believer is to judge himself. You are to be both the judge and the judged, for "if we would judge ourselves, we should not be judged" (v. 31).

If, when you examine yourself, you find yourself guilty and consequently unworthy, you are to confess your sin and correct the wrong. Merely to refrain from partaking of the Communion is no solution. There is but one wise course to follow: self-judgment, confession, correction, and participation.

The Communion service is a very solemn occasion, for unworthy participation will bring about guilt, damnation, and sickness. However, when you carefully follow the divine directives it becomes a blessed and necessary means of producing a proper attitude of remembrance of Christ and his cross, an atmosphere of harmony in the church, and spiritual and physical well-being in the members.

There is yet another significance to the Lord's Supper. Jesus said, "I will not drink henceforth of this fruit of the vine, until that day when I drink it new with you in my Father's kingdom" (Matthew 26:29).

The Communion is a reminder that we have an appointment with Jesus in the heavenly Kingdom. While we eat the bread and drink the cup in the Communion service, our Lord abstains from the fruit of the vine until we all will partake together in that great Communion service in heaven.

For many long centuries the Jews reminded one another that someday they would return to their land by repeating the motto, "Tomorrow in Jerusalem." The Christian, too, longs for his own land, and he reminds himself and his fellow believers with the promise of the Lord's Supper "until that day."

5 Be Filled With the Spirit

In a church in Cleveland, Ohio, the sermon had ended, and many of the people were praying at the altar. One teenage girl was praying fluently in Spanish and asking the Lord not to come until she could become a missionary. It was an odd prayer, and it especially seemed strange to the missionary speaker of the evening to hear a North American girl praying with such apparent ease in such a perfect Andean accent.

The missionary asked the pastor about the girl and learned she did not speak Spanish. She was from an Italian family, and her mother was present in the meeting. When the missionary asked the mother about her daughter, she replied, "Speak Spanish? She don't even speak Italian!"

Afterward, he spoke to the girl in Spanish, and she was unable to respond even to simple greetings. At a summer youth camp she had felt called to missionary service, and now she had spoken in an unknown language and asked the Lord to tarry long enough for her to fulfill her calling.

To what may we attribute such a miracle? The answer is clear to anyone well acquainted with New

Testament Christianity. She was a Spirit-filled person engaged in the apostolic experience of speaking in other tongues.

Her prayer, although not understood by herself or by most of those around her, was not the pronunciation of nonsensical syllables, as some critics might have suspected, but was in structured language and expressed her own deepest feelings to God.

A Wonderful Opportunity

One of the most delightful revelations awaiting you is the good news about the Spirit-filled life. To be filled with the Holy Spirit is a wonderful opportunity that will enrich your life and make you an effective witness for Christ.

On the Day of Pentecost, the 120 first Christians "were all with one accord in one place. And suddenly there came a sound from heaven as of a rushing mighty wind, and it filled all the house where they were sitting. And there appeared unto them cloven tongues like as of fire, and it sat upon each of them. And they were all filled with the Holy Ghost, and began to speak with other tongues, as the Spirit gave them utterance" (Acts 2:1-4).

When a large crowd of people gathered to see and hear what was happening, Peter preached an evangelistic sermon, "and the same day there were added unto them about three thousand souls" (Acts 2:41).

In Peter's altar call, he said, "Repent, and be baptized every one of you in the name of Jesus Christ for the remission of sins, and ye shall receive the gift of the Holy Ghost. For the promise is unto you, and to your children, and to all that are afar off, even as many as the Lord our God shall call" Acts 2:38,39).

There are several important principles expressed in Peter's statement: (1) There is a definite Biblical sequence of repentance, water baptism, and the baptism in the Holy Spirit; (2) the baptism in the Holy Spirit is promised to every believer who repents and is baptized; and (3) this promise will remain valid as long as the Lord our God calls for new believers.

The Day of Pentecost was not the only recorded case of the infilling of the Holy Spirit in the New Testament. In Acts 4:31 "they were all filled with the Holy Ghost, and they spake the word of God with boldness." After Philip had preached in Samaria, Peter and John joined him. "Then laid they their hands on them, and they received the Holy Ghost" (Acts 8:17).

When Peter preached to the house of Cornelius, "the Holy Ghost fell on all them which heard the word . . . For they heard them speak with tongues, and magnify God" (Acts 10:44,46). A few years later at Ephesus, "when Paul had laid his hands upon them, the Holy Ghost came on them; and they spake with tongues, and prophesied" (Acts 19:6).

Spirit-filled living was intended for the Early Church and for the church of all ages including our own.

WHY BE FILLED WITH THE SPIRIT?

When Jesus preached in the synagogue at Nazareth, He read His text from Isaiah 61:1,2, "The Spirit of the Lord is upon me, because. . . ." (Luke 4:18). Just as there was a "because" for the Holy Spirit in the life of Christ, there is a reason for the Holy Spirit in your life.

His purpose in Christ's life was clear: "Because he hath anointed me to preach the gospel to the poor; he hath sent me to heal the brokenhearted, to preach deliverance to the captives, and recovering of sight to the blind, to set at liberty them that are bruised, to preach the acceptable year of the Lord" (Luke 4:18,19). From start to finish, the Spirit's purpose in the life of Christ was to enable Him for service in the interest of advancing the Kingdom.

The Spirit's purpose in your life is very similar. While there are several related purposes, by far the greatest is enablement for Christian service. The last thing Jesus told His disciples before He ascended into heaven was, "But ye shall receive power, after that the Holy Ghost is come upon you: and ye shall be witnesses unto me both in Jerusalem, and in all Judea, and in Samaria, and unto the uttermost part of the earth" (Acts 1:8).

You should note three basic concepts: *power, witnesses,* and *scope.* This power is not normal human power, but a supernatural, miraculous force imparted by the Holy Ghost for Christian service. You will become a witness as a manifestation of the enduement with power. To speak of Christ becomes as natural as breathing. It will be neither forced nor feigned, but will occur as a natural manifestation of the power that is within you.

The scope of your witness will be worldwide, for you will love all men for whom Christ died and to whom He sends His church. You will participate in local evangelization, the spreading of the gospel throughout your own nation, and the preaching of the good news of Christ to the whole world. Your life will be characterized by an intense passion for local, home, and foreign missions.

ENRICHMENT FOR YOUR LIFE

Besides giving you power for Christian service, the Holy Spirit will enrich your life. Obviously, when this is done, you will become a more effective witness.

The Holy Spirit will enrich your study life. "Howbeit when he, the Spirit of truth, is come, he will guide you into all truth: for he shall not speak of himself; but whatsoever he shall hear, that shall he speak: and he will show you things to come" (John 16:13).

The Holy Spirit will enrich your prayer life. "Likewise the Spirit also helpeth our infirmities: for we know not what we should pray for as we ought: but the Spirit itself maketh intercession for us with groanings which cannot be uttered" (Romans 8:26).

The Holy Spirit will enrich your emotional life. "For the kingdom of God is not meat and drink; but righteousness, and peace, and joy in the Holy Ghost" (Romans 14:17). "Thou hast loved righteousness, and hated iniquity; therefore God, even thy God, hath anointed thee with the oil of gladness above thy fellows" (Hebrews 1:9).

The Holy Spirit will enrich your physical life. "But if the Spirit of him that raised up Jesus from the dead dwell in you, he that raised up Christ from the dead shall also quicken your mortal bodies by his Spirit that dwelleth in you" (Romans 8:11).

HOW TO RECEIVE THE SPIRIT

Before the Holy Spirit can endue you with power and enrich your life, He first must be received. The baptism in the Holy Spirit is a gift available to all who meet the conditions, but each individual must receive the experience for himself.

Of course, you experienced the work of the Holy Spirit when you accepted Christ as your Saviour, but the baptism in the Spirt is an experience separate from regeneration.

The baptism in the Holy Spirit is a definite experience that takes place at a recognizable moment of time subsequent to conversion and usually after water baptism. It does not occur inevitably, but comes only to those who actively seek it. Jesus told His disciples, "And, behold, I send the promise of my Father upon you: but tarry ye in the city of Jerusalem until ye be endued with power from on high" (Luke 24:49).

The baptism in the Holy Spirit comes to those who claim their divine promise and earnestly seek it as a personal experience. The first Christians to be filled with the Spirit "all continued with one accord in prayer and supplication" (Acts 1:14). Although some people are filled with little seeking, most tarry for the experience. Yet each must bring himself into a state of being with one accord with other Christians, and must pray quite earnestly to the point of supplication.

What are the conditions for receiving the Spirit? First, the Spirit is given to those who ask. "How much more shall your heavenly Father give the Holy Spirit to them that ask him?" (Luke 11:13). Certainly God will not force a gift on anyone, for to do so would violate man's freedom of choice. God simply announces the availability of the gift and places it within reach of all who ask.

Second, the Spirit is given to those who repent and are baptized. "Repent, and be baptized . . . and ye shall receive the gift of the Holy Ghost" (Acts 2:38). While it may appear at first glance that all who repent and are baptized receive the gift, this is not the case. Meeting these conditions only qualifies men to receive. The Samaritan converts of Acts 8 had met both conditions; yet, "he [the Holy Spirit] was fallen upon none of them" (Acts 8:16).

Why do some who have repented and been baptized fail to receive the gift of the Holy Spirit? The fault is not with God, but with man. Generally, the failure to receive may be traced to a lack of knowledge, to unbelief, or to misunderstanding of the truth.

Third, the Spirit is given to those who obey God. "And we are his witnesses of these things; and so is also the Holy Ghost, whom God hath given to them that obey him" (Acts 5:32). Obedience is always a prerequisite for receiving from God.

The act of receiving may occur in a variety of ways. The first Christians on the Day of Pentecost received while they were sitting, after they had prayed "in one accord" for 10 days (see Acts 2:2). The Samaritans received after Peter and John prayed for them and laid their hands on them (see Acts 8:15-17). Cornelius and his household received while Peter was preaching (see Acts 10:44). The Ephesians received after Paul had enlightened them, baptized them in water, and laid hands upon them (see Acts 19:1-6).

The variety in the Biblical examples shows there is no set pattern for receiving the Spirit. This is well supported by present-day experience. Some receive while alone in prayer, some at an altar or in a prayer room, and some when hands are laid on them. Place or position are of little consequence.

In three of the five Biblical cases, the apostles laid hands on these who received. In most cases, the practice should be done by ministers or mature Christians.

How to Know You Are Filled

When you fill the fuel tank of your car, there are two kinds of evidence of the filling. First, the gauges on the car and the fuel pump indicate the fact. Then the continued operation of the car confirms it. Although we must not press the analogy much beyond this point, you also will note two kinds of evidence of the baptism in the Holy Spirit.

The first evidence is that you will speak in other tongues. That is, you will pray in a language unknown to you. Strange as it may seem, it was a common occurrence in the Early Church, and it has been revived among Pentecostal and Charismatic Christians today.

On the Day of Pentecost, "they were all filled with the Holy Ghost, and began to speak with other tongues, as the Spirit gave them utterance" (Acts 2: 4). As we have seen, the early Christians also spoke in tongues at the house of Cornelius and in Ephesus. Paul wrote to the Corinthians, "For he that speaketh in an unknown tongue speaketh not unto men, but unto God" (1 Corinthians 14:2), and "I thank my God, I speak in tongues more than ye all" (1 Corinthians 14:18).

The Assemblies of God says that speaking in other tongues is the initial physical evidence that the believer has been baptized in the Holy Spirit. It is not the only evidence, but it is a vital sign to the believer and to the church.

The long-range evidence includes the whole development of the Christian life. "But the fruit of the Spirit is love, joy, peace, long-suffering, gentleness, goodness, faith, meekness, temperance" (Galatians 5:22,23). Some may argue that those who have not been baptized in the Holy Spirit may demonstrate these characteristics. That is true, but the Spirit-filled life will attain an intensification of all the best qualities of man.

Another major evidence is evangelism. The Spirit-filled Christian will have an intense desire to be a witness for Jesus Christ, for Jesus said, "But ye shall receive power, after that the Holy Ghost is come upon you: and ye shall be witnesses unto me" (Acts 1:8).

MAINTAIN THE EXPERIENCE

The baptism in the Holy Spirit is like the launching of a ship into a mighty ocean. While the launching is important, it is only the beginning of an adventurous voyage beyond the shallow waters along the shore.

The same people who were baptized in the Spirit in Acts 2:4 were refilled in Acts 4:23-31. There is one initial filling, but there are many returns to the fountain of blessing.

Paul's writings contain numerous instructions for maintaining the Spirit-filled life.

1. *Walk in the Spirit.* "Walk in the Spirit, and ye shall not fulfil the lusts of the flesh" (Galatians 5:16).

2. *Sow to the Spirit.* "But he that soweth to the Spirit shall of the Spirit reap life everlasting" (Galatians 6:8).

3. *Maintain unity.* "Endeavoring to keep the unity of the Spirit in the bond of peace" (Ephesians 4:3).

4. *Avoid grieving the Spirit.* "And grieve not the Holy Spirit of God" (Ephesians 4:30).

5. *Meditate on the Lord.* "Speaking to yourselves in psalms and hymns and spiritual songs, singing and making melody in your heart to the Lord" (Ephesians 5:19).

6. *Give thanks to God.* "Giving thanks always for all things unto God and the Father in the name of our Lord Jesus Christ" (Ephesians 5:20).

7. *Practice submission.* "Submitting yourselves one to another in the fear of God" (Ephesians 5:21).

8. *Pray in the Spirit.* "Praying always with all prayer and suppplication in the Spirit" (Ephesians 6:18). "I thank my God, I speak in tongues more than ye all" (1 Corinthians 14:18).

9. *Yield to the Spirit.* "Quench not the Spirit" (1 Thessalonians 5:19).

10. *Keep your experience up-to-date.* "Neglect not the gift that is in thee" (1 Timothy 4:14). "Wherefore I put thee in remembrance that thou stir up the gift of God, which is in thee by the putting on of my hands" (2 Timothy 1:6).

If you have not yet received this gift from God, do not become discouraged. Some people yield to the Spirit's control more easily than do others, so judge your experience only by the Word of God. Do not be afraid to yield to the Spirit, particularly when praying with a group of Spirit-filled people. If someone should lay hands upon you and pray for you, receive it as from God and let the Lord fill you with His Spirit.

Above all, do not take the word of others that you have been filled with the Spirit. When it happens, you will know it beyond any doubt. You will speak in other tongues and feel a great effluence of love for Jesus Christ.

6 Act Like a Christian

In a high school assembly the teachers were entertaining the students with their talents. Some sang songs from their own school days, and others played instruments or recited poetry.

One mathematics teacher, whom no one suspected of having musical talent, gave a beautiful performance on the violin. He closed his eyes and played the instrument with such apparent abandon that the whole student body was deeply moved.

Toward the end of the piece he paused to scratch his ear. Yet, the music continued! Again, he stopped to tune one of the strings, and still the music went on. The students howled with laughter when somebody pulled back the curtain and revealed the school's first-chair violinist with his instrument.

Such antics may be very funny in a school program, but in everyday life an obvious inconsistency between what you are and what you profess to be can lead to terrible tragedy.

Let no one say of you that your actions speak so loudly that people cannot hear what you say.

You are not saved by your own works, but by God's grace through Jesus Christ; yet, you will begin to alter your behavior after you accept Christ and will conform to certain standards of the Christian faith. As a tree may be identified by its fruit, so also will you be recognized as a Christian. Jesus said, "Ye shall know them by their fruits. Do men gather grapes of thorns, or figs of thistles? Even so every good tree bringeth forth good fruit; but a corrupt tree bringeth forth evil fruit" (Matthew 7:16,17).

STANDARDS OF CONDUCT

Can you really tell a Christian by the way he acts? The answer is a very definite *yes*. Although it is possible for some sinners to act like Christians, it is not possible for true Christians to act like sinners. The Christian faith has a definite standard of conduct required by God and expressed quite naturally in the sincere Christian life-style.

You must consider two basic factors for determining your pattern of behavior: (1) whether your action or attitude pleases God, and (2) whether it rightly influences the world toward God.

At this point, you must distinguish between divine morality and social ethics. God has laid down certain rules of behavior that He expects His children to follow. For example, He said, "Thou shalt not kill" (Exodus 20:13), which you must obey or face eternal judgment. The Bible teaches you to love your neighbor as much as you love yourself. This is a Biblical standard of conduct.

On the other hand, human society lays down its own standards of behavior. Some of these standards are called laws, and are set for the mutual good of the members of the community. For example, society says, "Thou shalt not drive down the middle of the road." A Christian will keep the laws of his community and his land so long as those laws do not conflict with the standards of conduct expressed clearly in the Bible.

Another kind of human standards is called social mores. These are rules of behavior required socially within a particular culture. Some Amazon Indian boys wear feathered headdresses that would seem very strange anywhere else in the world. Americans are expected to eat with the fork in the right hand, so that after cutting your meat you have to switch the knife and fork. Europeans and South Americans think this is very funny to watch, for they keep the knife in the right hand and eat with the fork in the left. Although as a Christian you will try to keep whatever social requirements best express your testimony to your community, you must recognize that such rules of etiquette cannot effect your eternal salvation.

Some social rules are difficult to analyze, for a Christian cannot separate himself from the society of which he is an integral part. You always must ask what your actions or attitudes mean within a particular cultural context, for as a Christian you must seek to be kind and polite and not cause misunderstandings about the motives of your conduct. A true Christian will act and dress in the manner that best allows him to be a witness of the gospel of Christ.

You will not stray far from correct conduct if you ask:

What is the real motive for my behavior?
What does the Bible say about my conduct?
How will God interpret what I am about to do?
How will other people interpret my actions?
What will be the result of such behavior?

When Solomon's temple was constructed, the cornerstones had to be laid with great precision because they set the standard for the entire building. They determined the direction of the building, governed its lines, and influenced its symmetry. If a cornerstone were off even a fraction of an inch, the entire building would be affected.

For similar reasons, Christ our Cornerstone must set the standard for the church and rule over it. He does this by His written Word, the Bible.

The Bible is the Word of God, the infallible rule of faith and conduct. In the Bible God projects the unchangeable standards in principle, precept, and example.

Although a Christian will try to be a cooperative member of human society, he recognizes that his true standards are not made by man, but by God. When Jesus was on earth, the Jews had substituted their own traditions for the ordinances of God; and Jesus told the religious leaders, "Thus have ye made the commandment of God of none effect by your tradition" (Matthew 15:6).

The purpose of Biblical standards is not to legislate righteousness, for real righteousness must come from the heart. Rather, such standards of conduct are a means of communicating the knowledge of what is or is not acceptable to God. "These things write I unto thee . . . that thou mayest know how thou oughtest to behave thyself" (1 Timothy 3:14,15).

And in This Corner . . .

As a young Christian, you will soon discover that your life is the arena of a life-and-death struggle.

You have become a "new creature" in Christ, but the old nature still wants to take over your life.

There are two deadly enemies engaged in mortal combat. The flesh is warring against the spirit, and the spirit against the flesh. Someone has called it "the conflict within." You can overcome the demands of the flesh if you will be filled with the Spirit of God and deny the fleshly lusts. "But if ye through the Spirit do mortify the deeds of the body, ye shall live" (Romans 8:13). "This I say then, Walk in the Spirit, and ye shall not fulfil the lust of the flesh" (Galatians 5:16).

The Bible speaks of the old man and the new man. "That ye put off concerning the former conversation the old man, which is corrupt according to the deceitful lusts; and be renewed in the spirit of your mind; and that ye put on the new man, which after God is created in righteousness and true holiness" (Ephesians 4:22-24).

It is important to realize that the old man and new man are not two forces outside yourself. You have been changed by Jesus Christ, born to your true destiny as a child of God; but your old nature still calls you strongly to return to your old habits, attitudes, desires, and sins. Your conflict is your own battle, the struggle between your own old worldly nature and new heavenly character.

By putting down the old man and letting the new man dominate, you free yourself from the old life and enter fully into the new.

In theology we speak of man as a free moral agent, meaning he is "a being that is capable of those actions that have a moral quality, and which can properly be denominated good or evil in a moral sense" (*A Theological Dictionary*, Charles Buck, 1826).

What this means is that you have in your power to do good or to do evil. Now that you have become a moral person by the grace and forgiveness of God, continue to live a moral life of the highest Christian standards.

For further study in the required behavior of the Christian life, read 1 Corinthians 6:9,10; Galatians 5:19-23; Ephesians 4:25-32; Colossians 3:5-25; and Titus 2:1-12. The standard of behavior for the believer is the list of works attributed by the Scriptures to the new man. To fall short of these is to fall short of pleasing God.

How a Christian Talks

Nothing more quickly and more accurately reflects the inward state of man than his speech. "For out of the abundance of the heart the mouth speaketh" (Matthew 12:34).

As it was with Christ, so it is with the Christian. "And they watched him . . . that they might take hold of his words" (Luke 20:20). Likewise, as it was with Christ, so let it be with each of us. "And they could not take hold of his words before the people" (Luke 20:26).

James recognized the importance of the Christian's domination over his tongue. "Behold, we put bits in the horses' mouths, that they may obey us; and we turn about their whole body. Behold also the ships, which though they be so great, and are driven of fierce winds, yet are they turned about with a very small helm, whithersoever the governor listeth. Even so the tongue is a little member, and boasteth great things. Behold, how great a matter a little fire kin-dieth! And the tongue is a fire . . . and it is set on fire of hell" (James 3:3-6).

A Christian will be recognized by his speech. When the apostles first spoke to the Jewish leaders after Pentecost, the high priest and his men "took knowledge of them that they had been with Jesus" (Acts 4:13).

You should be known both by what you say and what you will not say. For example, a real Christian will not slander anyone or speak evil of someone not present. He will not be known for his sharpness or bitterness of tongue. Jude spoke of people "having not the Spirit" as "murmurers, complainers, walking after their own lusts; and their mouth speaketh great swelling words" (Jude 16). A Christian will not be a gossip, for the Bible speaks of those who are "not only idle, but tattlers also and busybodies, speaking things which they ought not" (1 Timothy 5:13).

One thing that will identify you as a Christian will be the absence of swearing or swear-based slang from your vocabulary. The Bible says, "Let no corrupt communication proceed out of your mouth, but that which is good to the use of edifying, that it may minister grace unto the hearers" (Ephesians 4:29).

It goes on to say, "Let all bitterness, and wrath, and anger, and clamor, and evil speaking, be put away from you, with all malice: and be ye kind one to another, tender-hearted, forgiving one another, even as God for Christ's sake hath forgiven you" (vv. 31,32).

A Christian is to speak with grace and carefulness, for the Bible says, "Let your speech be always with grace, seasoned with salt, that ye may know how ye ought to answer every man" (Colossians 4:6).

We must remember that we represent Christ in all we say and do. Therefore, we must speak the truth, must give the world sound doctrine (see Titus 2:1), and must not forget that the world is always watching and listening.

W. E. Norris wrote in *Thirlby Hall*:

> "If you your lips would keep from slips,
>   Five things observe with care:
> To whom you speak, of whom you speak,
>   And how, and when, and where."

HOW A CHRISTIAN DRESSES

Standards for Christian dress and adornment have been a subject of controversy over the centuries. Sometimes so much attention has been given to the subject that people have disregarded other important standards of Christian conduct. The basic problem seems to be that styles and cultural patterns change, and fixed Christian opinions on dress codes soon become antiquated. There is no unchanging Christian uniform common to all ages and all cultures. Rather, the Christians of each time and place must reinterpret the Biblical standards in the light of their own social customs and culture.

A sincere Christian will dress and act in whatever ways best witness for Christ within his society. He will dress modestly and will not be known for his inordinate display of his wealth (see 1 Timothy 2:9,10; 1 Peter 3:1-5).

Neither boastful extravagance nor plain shabbiness of dress will attract the world to Jesus Christ. In general, a Christian's apparel will be known for its conservative tone, its modesty, and its representation of the seriousness of the Christian message. Its style may be contemporary and its quality high, but its purposes, beyond those of warmth and covering, will be to express the Christian message and identify the messenger.

Our best example may be found in Jesus Christ himself, whose robe, though apparently simple, was of sufficient quality that the Roman soldiers cast lots for it at the foot of the cross.

HOW A CHRISTIAN SHOULD THINK

The way we use our minds determines the way we go, for our actions are but the embodiment of our thoughts. Paul said, "Finally, brethren, whatsoever things are true, whatsoever things are honest, whatsoever things are just, whatsoever things are pure, whatsoever things are lovely, whatsoever things are of good report; if there be any virtue, and if there be any praise, think on these things" (Philippians 4:8).

While God has made provision for your victorious thought-life, it is certain that you in turn must fill your mind with good, meditate on the things of God, resist the devil's attempts to corrupt your mind, associate with good men, avoid companionship with evil men, stay away even from the appearance of evil, and choose wholesome and constructive reading material.

The purpose of right conduct is right relationship to God and men. As a Christian, you are living in this world, but you are a citizen of the world to come. You are an eternal child of God temporarily housed in the body of an earthly man. Walk worthy of your high calling, for heaven, hell, and this present world are watching your progress.

7 Giving From the Heart

There is a principle that is hard to understand and yet so important to the Christian faith that without it you will fail to reach full maturity. The essence of this law is: Before you may truly have for yourself you must give for others.

Many preachers and writers have echoed this principle through the ages. Charles Spurgeon put it this way: "Giving is true having." George Granville said, "What we frankly give, forever is our own." Victor Hugo said it, "As the purse is emptied the heart is filled." Jesus said, "It is more blessed to give than to receive" (Acts 20:35). And He said, "Give, and it shall be given unto you; good measure, pressed down, and shaken together, and running over, shall men give into your bosom. For with the same measure that ye mete withal it shall be measured to you again" (Luke 6:38).

The highest example of this principle comes from God himself. "For God so loved the world, that he gave his only begotten Son, that whosoever believeth in him should not perish, but have everlasting life" (John 3:16). God first gave His Son so we might have life, which will result in His having a saved people in heaven. The giving comes back to the giver.

There are four kinds of Christian giving. First, a child of God gives himself to the full service of his Heavenly Father and Lord. He responds to divine personality and authority with an unquestioning devotion to God and His infallible will. Second, he will give of himself for the good of his fellowmen. Third, he gives a tenth of his financial earnings, his tithe, for the operation and ministry of the church. And, fourth, he contributes from his means for the help of mankind and the propagation of the gospel.

The Christian life has two distinct sides. On the one hand you receive from God and partake of His benefits. On the other, you recognize the Lordship of God and your responsibility to apply all your resources to the furthering of His kingdom. Paul spoke of "God, whose I am, and whom I serve" (Acts 27:23).

The care of a Christian for his financial responsibilities to God through His church is called Christian stewardship. Its basis is not so much in matters of money as in divine ownership of you and all your resources. "What! know ye not that your body is the temple of the Holy Ghost which is in you, which ye have of God, and ye are not your own? For ye are bought with a price" (1 Corinthians 6:19,20).

As a steward, you are answerable to the Master for all He has placed in your hand—time, talents, truth, and treasure. The one requirement is faithfulness. "Let a man so account of us, as of the ministers of Christ, and stewards of the mysteries of God. Moreover it is required in stewards that a man be found faithful" (1 Corinthians 4:1,2).

In subsequent chapters we will consider your responsibility toward Christian doctrine and your own involvement of time and talents in world evangelization. Let us for the present think of your stewardship of finances. Once you learn the blessedness of this practice, you will experience little difficulty with the other areas of stewardship.

Why You Must Give

Jesus said, "Lay not up for yourselves treasures upon earth. . . . But lay up for yourselves treasures in heaven . . . for where your treasure is, there will your heart be also" (Matthew 6:19-21).

Man's basic problems center in his heart. God desires man's heart above all else, and He knows that if He has a man's treasure He has his heart also. But Christian giving is more than this; it is a reflection of God's generosity toward man. It is in the very nature of Christian love to give, "For God so loved the world, that he gave" (John 3:16). Jesus Christ "gave himself a ransom for all" (1 Timothy 2:6). The Holy Spirit manifests gifts to men (see 1 Corinthians 12:8-10).

You must give because you are a child of God and must demonstrate your relationship to your Heavenly Father. To give is now your nature. Do not complain that He asks this of you, for no amount of giving on your part can begin to compare with the worth of eternal life or the value of all else you have received from Him.

Your gift to God comes back in His benefits to you.

Giving is a form of worship. Anything you give to God and His work is an offering of praise. It is an act of worship whereby your love is expressed through a practical, tangible means.

Giving enriches your life. The cheerful and sincere giver places himself in a most favorable position for God's further blessings, "for God loveth a cheerful giver" (2 Corinthians 9:7).

The solid foundation for true enrichment is liberality. "There is that scattereth, and yet increaseth; and there is that withholdeth more than is meet, but it tendeth to poverty. The liberal soul shall be made fat: and he that watereth shall be watered also himself" (Proverbs 11:24,25). "But this I say, He which soweth sparingly shall reap also sparingly; and he which soweth bountifully shall reap also bountifully" (2 Corinthians 9:6).

It is strangely and wonderfully true that the act of giving increases our capacity for receiving from the hand of God, while tightfistedness produces the exact opposite result.

Giving sustains the work of God. God's method of providing for the financial need of His cause is through His children and their resources.

God has always called on His people to support His ministers. The Old Testament priesthood was sustained through tithes and offerings. When the people failed, the priestly functions were curtailed and the judgments of God fell (see Malachi 3:7-11).

In the New Testament order, giving is not so much a matter of law, but of privilege and nature. Yet, the New Testament says, "If we have sown unto you spiritual things, is it a great thing if we shall reap your carnal things? . . . Do ye not know that they which minister about holy things live of the things of the temple? and they which wait at the altar are partakers with the altar? Even so hath the Lord ordained that they which preach the gospel should live of the gospel" (1 Corinthians 9:11-14).

As you give to the church, you in turn benefit from the church you help to support.

Giving helps prevent covetousness. Of all the sins, one of the most subtle is covetousness. As heathen men make gods of wood, stone, or metal, so many men make their gods of money and other possessions. All sins are dangerous, but that of covetous idolatry is particularly damning. It is like a lamprey, which fastens itself to a fish and saps it of its very life.

There is nothing wrong with money itself; it is what we do with it and what we let it do to us that causes us difficulties. It is the love of money, not the money itself that gives us problems (see 1 Timothy 6:10).

The sin of covetousness cannot take root where the spirit of liberality is flourishing. Let Christian liberality abound, and covetousness will perish. It is a Biblical law.

PRINCIPLES OF CHRISTIAN GIVING

The financial needs of the church find their happy solution not in high-pressured appeals or in fundraising gimmicks, but in Christian giving based on Scriptural principles. Let us consider six such principles of giving.

1. *Stewardship based on divine ownership.* You must recognize that God owns you and all you possess. In fact, everything you think you own came from His hand. You are not really the owner of your possessions, but the steward of God's possessions. You have a sacred responsibility to handle His finances well, for you will be called upon to give an account.

2. *Debt based on service rendered.* When the plumber is called into the home to repair a leaky waterline, he renders a service. In turn, the home-owner recognizes his debt and willingly pays the bill. You, too, must recognize yourself a debtor because of what God has done for you.

You cannot repay the Lord for His service, but you are nonetheless indebted. In recognition of this debt you are to present your body a living sacrifice (see Romans 12:1,2) for the purpose of getting the glorious gospel to all men. Involved in this is your whole-hearted support of the church's effort to reach the lost.

3. *Receiving based on giving.* As we have seen, this is the principle of reaping based on sowing (see 2 Corinthians 9:6). It is increase based on investment.

Sadly enough, there are unscrupulous people who abuse this principle. They promise prosperity if you will support their cause, thus attempting to convince you that you will grow rich because you give. The Bible makes no promise of wealth or luxury, but rather says to those who support the church and its missionary cause, "But my God shall supply all your need according to his riches in glory by Christ Jesus" (Philippians 4:19).

4. *Acceptability based on willingness.* God does not evaluate your offering on the basis of amount, but on your willingness to share what you have. To Jesus, the widow's mite, given willingly and gladly, is far more acceptable than the rich man's costly gift if bestowed grudgingly.

God does not expect you to give more than you are able, but He desires you to give willingly according

70

to your ability. "For if there be first a willing mind, it is accepted according to that a man hath, and not according to that he hath not" (2 Corinthians 8:12).

5. *Systematic giving based on income.* Both the Old and New Testaments teach systematic giving. In the Old Testament the plain injunction was, "And all the tithe of the land, whether of the seed of the land, or of the fruit of the tree, is the Lord's: it is holy unto the Lord" (Leviticus 27:30).

The New Testament principle is, "Upon the first day of the week [that is, systematically] let every one of you lay by him in store, as God hath prospered him [according to his income]" (1 Corinthians 16:2).

In church financing, God wills that everyone share equally, according to his means. "For I mean not that other men be eased, and ye burdened: but by an equality, that now at this time your abundance may be a supply for their want, that their abundance also may be a supply for your want: that there may be equality" (2 Corinthians 8:13,14).

There is no more equitable, fair, and systematically well-balanced way to support the church than the Biblical tithe system. To tithe, you simply give back to God one-tenth of your income. That tenth is not yours; it is His. In addition, God expects you to go beyond mere tithing to give offerings out of the abundance of your heart and purse.

6. *Worthiness based on service rendered.* God does not charge for His services of love. Yet, if you have received of His bountiful blessings you will want to offer something in return. God's church and its ministries must be supported if they are to function properly. Jesus said, "For the laborer is worthy of his hire" (Luke 10:7). And, as we have seen, Paul said,

"Even so hath the Lord ordained that they which preach the gospel should live of the gospel" (1 Corinthians 9:14).

HOW TO GIVE

The church is not supported by the principles of giving, but by the practice of giving. Theoretical dollars fill no offering plates. At some point, you must come down from the lofty heights of theory and face the responsibility of giving real money in an actual church offering.

Perhaps the following questions and answers will help you get started.

Q: Who should give in a church offering?

A: All, without exception. Everyone is invited to participate and thus lay the foundation for God's abundant provision (see Philippians 4:19).

Q: To whom should you give?

A: Your first obligation is to your home church. All of your tithes and most of your offerings should be given there, for you share with the other members the responsibility of supporting your pastor and the church ministries.

The Bible says, "Bring ye all the tithes into the storehouse, that there may be meat in mine house, and prove me now herewith, saith the Lord of hosts, if I will not open you the windows of heaven, and pour you out a blessing, that there shall not be room enough to receive it" (Malachi 3:10).

In the Assemblies of God we teach that the "storehouse" is your local church. The tithes and offerings go into a church fund from which the congregation may care for its obligations, including pastors' salaries, buildings, maintenance, utilities, and other expenses. In addition, we ask every believer to give meaningfully toward the evangelization of the world.

Q: When should you give?

A: Many Christians make it a matter of principle to give something in every offering. However, it is the total giving and its comparative ratio to your earnings that matter. Most people give weekly or monthly, according to their pattern of income.

Q: How much should you give above your tithe?

A: Don't ask how little you can give, but how much you may accomplish for God. Every dollar you give represents a portion of your working hours. If you can't preach the gospel yourself, then make sure you give some of your time and talents so that others may preach and otherwise minister. Life is short; do all the good you can with what you have to give.

Q: How should you give?

A: If your church uses offering envelopes, use them so you will have a record of your giving. An annual statement from the church will help you with your tax reports. It is always wise for tax purposes to give by check. By all means, give systematically and faithfully as the Lord prospers you.

One church member asked, "Why do preachers always talk about money?" His pastor replied, "I wouldn't need to mention it if all the members would obey the Word of God."

8 The Fundamental Doctrines

"Why aren't our churches like those of the apostles' day?" asked a group of Bible school students in Topeka, Kansas, just before the Christmas vacation of the year 1900. "The early Christians were filled with the Holy Spirit and spoke with other tongues. They healed the sick and cast out devils. They had such power to preach that their whole world was challenged by the gospel."

"Because those things are not for us today," was the stock reply.

During the Christmas holidays, the students who remained at the school decided to test that old answer by actively seeking the baptism in the Holy Spirit. On January 1, 1901, after the students had "tarried" in prayer, a young woman, Agnes Ozman, was filled with the Holy Spirit and began to speak in other tongues, just as the apostles did on the Day of Pentecost. The other students also received during the next few days.

That event was the beginning of a great religious awakening that produced the Pentecostal Movement and had a profound effect on 20th-century Christianity.

As the largest Pentecostal church, the Assemblies of God has deeply moved this generation with its dynamic life, its apostolic doctrine, and its worldwide evangelization.

The Pentecostal form of Christianity is that theological position which calls for a complete return to the doctrines, the religious experiences, the basic practices, and the priorities of the Apostolic Church.

Now that you are a part of the Assemblies of God, you should consider yourself a Pentecostal Christian. Sometimes we describe ourselves as "full gospel," meaning that we believe all the teachings of the New Testament church.

The opening words of the first official minutes of our church in April, 1914, said, "For a number of years, God has been leading men to seek for a full apostolic gospel standard of experience and doctrine." That is still the best description of our beliefs.

STATEMENT OF FUNDAMENTAL TRUTHS

The Bible says that "they continued steadfastly in the apostles' doctrine and fellowship" (Acts 2:42). It is very important that you know the doctrines of your church so that you may closely identify yourself with its fellowship.

For this reason, we present to you the entire text of our church's Statement of Fundamental Truths, first formed in 1914 and last revised at the Dallas General Council in 1969.

The Bible is our all-sufficient rule for faith and practice. This Statement of Fundamental Truths is intended simply as a basis of fellowship among us (i.e., that we all speak the same thing, 1 Cor. 1:10; Acts 2:42). The phraseology employed in this Statement is not inspired or contended for, but the truth set forth is held to be essential to a Full Gospel ministry. No claim is made that it covers all Biblical truth, only that it covers our need as to these fundamental doctrines.

1. The Scriptures Inspired

The Scriptures, both the Old and New Testaments, are verbally inspired of God and are the revelation of God to man, the infallible, authoritative rule of faith and conduct (2 Tim. 3:15-17; 1 Thess. 2:13; 2 Peter 1:21).

2. The One True God

The one true God has revealed himself as the eternally self-existent "I AM," the Creator of heaven and earth and the Redeemer of mankind. He has further revealed himself as embodying the principles of relationship and association as Father, Son, and Holy Ghost (Deut. 6:4; Isa. 43:10,11; Matt. 28:19; Luke 3:22).

THE ADORABLE GODHEAD

(a) TERMS DEFINED

The terms "Trinity" and "persons," as related to the Godhead, while not found in the Scriptures, are words in harmony with Scripture, whereby we may convey to others our immediate understanding of the doctrine of Christ respecting the Being of God, as distinguished from "gods many and lords many." We therefore may speak with propriety of the Lord our God, who is One Lord, as a trinity or as one Being of three persons, and still be absolutely scriptural (examples, Matt. 28:19; 2 Cor. 13:14; John 14:16,17).

(b) DISTINCTION AND RELATIONSHIP IN THE GODHEAD

Christ taught a distinction of Persons in the Godhead which He expressed in specific terms of relationship, as Father, Son, and Holy Ghost, but that this distinction and relationship, as to its mode is *inscrutable* and *incomprehensible*, because *unexplained*. Luke 1:35; 1 Cor.

76

1:24; Matt. 11:25-27; 28:19; 2 Cor. 13:14; 1 John 1:3,4.

(C) UNITY OF THE ONE BEING OF FATHER, SON AND HOLY GHOST

Accordingly, therefore, there is *that* in the Son which constitutes Him *the Son* and not the Father; and there is *that* in the Holy Ghost which constitutes Him *the Holy Ghost* and not either the Father or the Son. Wherefore the Father is the Begetter, the Son is the Begotten, and the Holy Ghost is the one proceeding from the Father and the Son. Therefore, because these three persons in the Godhead are in a state of unity, there is but one Lord God Almighty and His name one. John 1:18; 15:26; 17:11,21; Zech. 14:9.

(D) IDENTITY AND COOPERATION IN THE GODHEAD

The Father, the Son, and the Holy Ghost are never *identical* as to *Person;* nor *confused* as to *relation;* nor *divided* in respect to the Godhead; nor *opposed* as to *cooperation.* The Son is *in* the Father and the Father is *in* the Son as to relationship. The Son is *with* the Father and the Father is *with* the Son, as to fellowship. The Father is not *from* the Son, but the Son is *from* the Father, as to authority. The Holy Ghost is *from* the Father and the Son proceeding, as to nature, relationship, cooperation and authority. Hence, neither Person in the Godhead either exists or works separately or independently of the others. John 5:17-30,32,37; John 8:17,18.

(E) THE TITLE, LORD JESUS CHRIST

The appellation, "Lord Jesus Christ," is a proper name. It is never applied, in the New Testament, either to the Father or to the Holy Ghost. It therefore belongs exclusively to the *Son of God.* Rom. 1:1-3,7; 2 John 3.

(F) THE LORD JESUS CHRIST, GOD WITH US

The Lord Jesus Christ, as to His divine and eternal nature, is the proper and only Begotten of the Father, but as to His human nature, He is the proper Son of Man. He is, therefore, acknowledged to be both God and man; who because He is God and man, is "Immanuel,"

God with us. Matt. 1:23; 1 John 4:2,10,14; Rev. 1:13,17.

(G) THE TITLE, SON OF GOD

Since the name "Immanuel" embraces both God and man in the one Person, our Lord Jesus Christ, it follows that the title, Son of God, describes His proper deity, and the title Son of Man, His proper humanity. Therefore, the title, Son of God, belongs to the *order of eternity*, and the title, Son of Man, to the *order of time*. Matt. 1:21-23; 2 John 3; 1 John 3:8; Heb. 7:3; 1:1-13.

(H) TRANSGRESSION OF THE DOCTRINE OF CHRIST

Wherefore, it is a transgression of the Doctrine of Christ to say that Jesus Christ derived the title, Son of God, solely from the fact of the incarnation, or because of His relation to the economy of redemption. Therefore, to deny that the Father is a real and eternal Father, and that the Son is a real and eternal Son is a denial of the distinction and relationship in the Being of God; a denial of the Father and the Son; and a displacement of the truth that Jesus Christ is come in the flesh. 2 John 9; John 1:1,2,14,18,29,49; 1 John 2:22,23; 4:1-5; Heb. 12:2.

(I) EXALTATION OF JESUS CHRIST AS LORD

The Son of God, our Lord Jesus Christ, having by himself purged our sins, sat down on the right hand of the Majesty on high; angels and principalities and powers having been made subject unto Him. And having been made both Lord and Christ, He sent the Holy Ghost that we, in the name of Jesus, might bow our knees and confess that Jesus Christ is Lord to the glory of God the Father until the end, when the Son shall become subject to the Father that God may be all in all. Heb. 1:3; 1 Peter 3:22; Acts 2:32-36; Rom. 14:11; 1 Cor. 15:24-28.

(J) EQUAL HONOR TO THE FATHER AND TO THE SON

Wherefore, since the Father has delivered all judgment unto the Son, it is not only the *express duty* of all in heaven and on earth to bow the knee, but it is an *unspeakable* joy in the Holy Ghost to ascribe unto the Son all the attributes of Deity, and to give Him all the honor and the glory contained in all the names and titles of the Godhead except those which express relationship (see paragraphs b, c, and d), and thus honor the Son even as we honor the Father. John 5:22, 23; 1 Peter 1:8; Rev. 5:6-14; Phil. 2:8,9; Rev. 7:9,10; 4:8-11.

3. The Deity of the Lord Jesus Christ

The Lord Jesus Christ is the eternal Son of God. The Scriptures declare:
(a) His virgin birth (Matt. 1:23; Luke 1:31,35).
(b) His sinless life (Heb. 7:26; 1 Peter 2:22).
(c) His miracles (Acts 2:22; 10:38).
(d) His substitutionary work on the cross (1 Cor. 15:3; 2 Cor. 5:21).
(e) His bodily resurrection from the dead (Matt. 28:6; Luke 24:39; 1 Cor. 15:4).
(f) His exaltation to the right hand of God (Acts 1:9,11; 2:33; Phil. 2:9-11; Heb. 1-3).

4. The Fall of Man

Man was created good and upright; for God said, "Let us make man in our image, after our likeness." However, man by voluntary transgression fell and thereby incurred not only physical death but also spiritual death, which is separation from God (Gen. 1:26,27; 2:17; 3:6; Rom. 5:12-19).

5. The Salvation of Man

Man's only hope of redemption is through the shed blood of Jesus Christ the Son of God.

(a) Conditions to Salvation

Salvation is received through repentance toward God and faith toward the Lord Jesus Christ. By the washing of regeneration and renewing of the Holy Ghost, being justified by grace through faith, man becomes an heir of God, according to the hope of eternal life (Luke 24:47; John 3:3; Rom. 10:13-15; Eph. 2:8; Titus 2:11; 3:5-7).

(b) The Evidences of Salvation

The inward evidence of salvation is the direct witness of the Spirit (Romans 8:16). The outward evidence to all men is a life of righteousness and true holiness (Eph. 4:24; Titus 2:12).

6. ORDINANCES OF THE CHURCH

(a) Baptism in Water

The ordinance of baptism by immersion is commanded in the Scriptures. All who repent and believe on Christ as Saviour and Lord are to be baptized. Thus they declare to the world that they have died with Christ and that they also have been raised with Him to walk in newness of life. (Matt. 28:19; Mark 16:16; Acts 10:47,48; Rom. 6:4).

(b) Holy Communion

The Lord's Supper, consisting of the elements—bread and the fruit of the vine—is the symbol expressing our sharing the divine nature of our Lord Jesus Christ (2 Peter 1:4); a memorial of His suffering and death (1 Cor. 11:26); and a prophecy of His second coming (1 Cor. 11:26); and is enjoined on all believers "till He come!"

7. THE BAPTISM IN THE HOLY GHOST

All believers are entitled to and should ardently expect and earnestly seek the promise of the Father, the baptism in the Holy Ghost and fire, according to the command of our Lord Jesus Christ. This was the normal experience of all in the early Christian Church. With it comes the enduement of power for life and service, the bestowment of the gifts and their uses in the work of the ministry (Luke 24:49; Acts 1:4,8; 1 Cor. 12:1-31). This experience is distinct from and subsequent to the experience of the new birth (Acts 8:12-17; 10:44-46; 11:14-16; 15:7-9). With the baptism in the Holy Ghost come such experiences as an overflowing fullness of the Spirit (John 7:37-39; Acts 4:8), a deepened reverence for God (Acts 2:43; Heb. 12:28), an intensified consecration to God and dedication to His work (Acts 2:42), and a more active love for Christ, for His Word, and for the lost (Mark 16:20).

8. THE EVIDENCE OF THE BAPTISM IN THE HOLY GHOST

The baptism of believers in the Holy Ghost is witnessed by the initial physical sign of speaking with other tongues as the Spirit of God gives them utterance (Acts 2:4). The speaking in tongues in this instance is the same in essence as the gift of tongues (1 Cor. 12:4-10,28), but different in purpose and use.

9. SANCTIFICATION

Sanctification is an act of separation from that which is evil, and of dedication unto God (Rom. 12:1,2; 1 Thess. 5:23; Heb. 13:12). The Scriptures teach a life of "holiness without which no man shall see the Lord" (Heb. 12:14). By the power of the Holy Ghost we are able to obey the command: "Be ye holy, for I am holy" (1 Peter 1:15,16).

Sanctification is realized in the believer by recognizing his identification with Christ in His death and resurrection, and by faith reckoning daily upon the fact of that union, and by offering every faculty continually to the dominion of the Holy Spirit (Rom.

6:1-11,13; 8:1,2,13; Gal. 2:20; Phil. 2:12,13; 1 Peter 1:5).

10. The Church and Its Mission

The Church is the Body of Christ, the habitation of God through the Spirit, with divine appointments for the fulfillment of her great commission. Each believer, born of the Spirit, is an integral part of the General Assembly and Church of the Firstborn, which are written in heaven (Ephesians 1:22,23; 2:22; Hebrews 12:23).

Since God's purpose concerning man is to seek and to save that which is lost, to be worshiped by man, and to build a body of believers in the image of His Son, the priority reason-for-being of the Assemblies of God as part of the Church is:

a. To be an agency of God for evangelizing the world (Acts 1:8; Matthew 28:19,20; Mark 16:15, 16).

b. To be a corporate body in which man may worship God (1 Corinthians 12:13).

c. To be a channel of God's purpose to build a body of saints being perfected in the image of His Son (Ephesians 4:11-16; 1 Corinthians 12:28; 1 Corinthians 14:12).

The Assemblies of God exists expressly to give continuing emphasis to this reason-for-being in the New Testament apostolic pattern by teaching and encouraging believers to be baptized in the Holy Spirit. This experience:

a. Enables them to evangelize in the power of the Spirit with accompanying supernatural signs (Mark 16:15-20; Acts 4:29-31; Hebrews 2:3,4).

b. Adds a necessary dimension to worshipful relationship with God (1 Corinthians 2:10-16; 1 Corinthians 12,13, and 14).

c. Enables them to respond to the full working of the Holy Spirit in expression of fruit and gifts and ministries as in New Testament times for the edifying of the body of Christ (Galatians 5:22-26; 1 Corinthians 14:12; Ephesians 4:11,12; 1 Corinthians 12:28; Colossians 1:29).

11. THE MINISTRY

A divinely called and scripturally ordained ministry has been provided by our Lord for the threefold purpose of leading the Church in: (1) Evangelization of the world (Mark 16:15-20), (2) Worship of God (John 4:23,24), (3) Building a body of saints being perfected in the image of His Son (Ephesians 4:11-16).

12. DIVINE HEALING

Divine healing is an integral part of the gospel. Deliverance from sickness is provided for in the atonement, and is the privilege of all believers (Isa. 53:4,5; Matt. 8:16,17; James 5:14-16).

13. THE BLESSED HOPE

The resurrection of those who have fallen asleep in Christ and their translation together with those who are alive and remain unto the coming of the Lord is the imminent and blessed hope of the church (1 Thess. 4:16,17; Rom. 8:23; Titus 2:13; 1 Cor. 15:51,52).

14. THE MILLENNIAL REIGN OF CHRIST

The second coming of Christ includes the rapture

of the saints, which is our blessed hope, followed by the visible return of Christ with His saints to reign on the earth for one thousand years (Zech. 14:5; Matt. 24:27,30; Rev. 1:7; 19:11-14; 20:1-6). This millennial reign will bring the salvation of national Israel (Ezek. 37:21,22; Zeph. 3:19,20; Rom. 11:26,27) and the establishment of universal peace (Isa. 11:6-9; Ps. 72:3-8; Micah 4:3,4).

15. THE FINAL JUDGMENT

There will be a final judgment in which the wicked dead will be raised and judged according to their works. Whosoever is not found written in the Book of Life, together with the devil and his angels, the beast and the false prophet, will be consigned to everlasting punishment in the lake which burneth with fire and brimstone, which is the second death (Matt. 25:46; Mark 9:43-48; Rev. 19:20; 20:11-15; 21:8).

16. THE NEW HEAVENS AND THE NEW EARTH

"We, according to His promise, look for new heavens and a new earth wherein dwelleth righteousness" (2 Peter 3:13; Rev. 21,22).[1]

[1] Copies of the Assemblies of God Statement of Fundamental Truths in pamphlet form are available from The General Council of the Assemblies of God, 1445 Boonville Avenue, Springfield, Missouri 65802.

9 The Security of Belonging

On a foreign mission field a young heathen woman told a missionary, "I want to marry a member of your church."

"And which one will you marry?" asked the missionary.

"Oh, any of them," she replied.

Perplexed at her answer, the missionary asked, "But if you don't know which to marry, how do you know you want to be the wife of one of our church members?"

She responded, "Because they say the members of your church don't beat their wives!"

The missionary could not speak for all who attended the church, but he could testify sincerely that she was right about the church members. He led the young lady to the Lord, and she eventually married a fine Christian youth.

Church membership is a very meaningful part of the Christian life. Its purposes and blessings go far beyond mere business meetings and records to become an important factor in the church's Christian witness in its community and the world.

You ought to join a local church, both for what the church can do for you and for what you can do for the church. It is vital to your interests to under-stand the advantages of church membership and the reasons for it.

The devil may use even well-meaning people to try to influence you to remain aloof from local-church responsibility; but remember that heaven itself keeps a membership roll. "And I saw the dead, small and great, stand before God; and the books were opened. . . . And whosoever was not found written in the book of life was cast into the lake of fire" (Revelation 20:12,15).

SIGN THE CHURCH ROLL

The idea of church membership is well supported both in the Old and New Testaments. In Numbers 1:1-2, God commanded Moses to make a careful record of all Israel according to their families. Moses did this, and at least a part of the record is preserved to this day.

Some people object to church membership on the basis of God's severe judgment on King David for numbering the people (see 1 Chronicles 21:4-17). But this must be understood in the light of David's motive, which was inspired by Satan. "And Satan stood up against Israel, and provoked David to num-ber Israel" (1 Chronicles 21:1). The king was tempted to take a special census so he could boast of his victories. The passage has nothing to do with church membership.

As the necessity for membership arose in the Early Church, the Holy Spirit led in the development of organizational structure. The 120 in the Upper Room held a business meeting to elect the successor to Judas Iscariot (see Acts 1:15-26). Another meeting of the membership took place in Acts 6:1-7, when the Early Church elected the first deacons.

From the beginning there was a clearly defined company of believers. "And the same day there were added unto them about three thousand souls" (Acts 2:41). "And they were all with one accord in Solomon's porch. And of the rest durst no man join himself to them: but the people magnified them. And believers were the more added to the Lord, multitudes both of men and women" (Acts 5:12-14). "And in those days, when the number of the disciples was multiplied . . . " (Acts 6:1).

The church faces an almost impossible task, that of total community and world evangelization. To accomplish its divinely ordered commission, the church must be united in purpose and in might. A loosely organized, poorly structured fellowship cannot possibly do God's task in the world.

A man, one time, gathered his sons together to demonstrate the value of unity. He took a twig and broke it easily. Then, he tried to break a bundle of twigs and could not do so. In this manner he taught them that in unity there is strength.

REASONS FOR MEMBERSHIP

Some of the reasons for church membership are similar to those for marriage. It binds people together in a lasting relationship, leads to responsible patterns of living, avoids the pitfalls of immoral behavior, and provides an environment for full human maturation.

Worship may be a spontaneous act by an individual or any group of believers, but worship reaches a high intensity and effectiveness when it is done by an organized group of church members who gather regularly and have shared together their sorrows and joys.

Another purpose of membership is that it produces a sense of belonging. Today's society is so mobile that many people do not know the true feeling of home. The attachment to a church family gives the individual believer this often missing element of being a part of a family of people who love him and remember him in prayer. Within this context the member responds with loyalty and responsibility.

Membership is necessary, too, for effective organization. Throughout the Bible we are shown a pattern of organization. God created a structured universe, organized down to its finest details. Israel was carefully organized into 12 tribes. The Levitical priesthood was organized. When Jesus fed the multitude, He had the people sit in orderly groups and be served by the disciples in an orderly fashion (see Mark 6:39,40).

A clearly defined membership is essential if the church is to select its officers, own and maintain its property, and conduct other business. Without a membership roster, church business is handled poorly; and important decisions can be made by marginally involved people who do not understand the business at hand and who most probably will not remain to live with the results of their decisions.

Membership also makes possible a united effort to spread the gospel. Much more is involved in Christianity than individual response to religion; the Christian faith is based on a "body" concept of the church whereby the believers become a single community of God-fearing, Christ-honoring, mutually loving, gospel-preaching people. Apart from careful organization, of which church membership is an integral part, the Assemblies of God could not have or maintain its mighty army of home and foreign missionaries, its thousands of mission stations, and its nearly 150 Bible schools around the world.

Nothing of value is created without the temper of discipline. Human initiative and talent are important, but it is the application of patience, correction, and strategy that produces the best results. Without membership, every man becomes a law unto himself. With an organized church roll, the congregation can establish standards of belief and conduct and thereby maintain its quality.

Finally, membership makes possible a statistical report. It allows the church to evaluate its progress, face its problems, and fortify its strengths. There are additional benefits, too. For example, the number of military chaplains a church denomination may have depends upon its number of members.

How to Become a Member

It's easy to apply. All Assemblies of God churches have membership application forms, which you may obtain simply by asking the pastor. Your application will be reviewed by the church board; and, if approved, you will be welcomed to membership in a public service. Many churches require you to take a class in the fundamental doctrines of the church.

If you transfer your membership from another church, you should ask your former pastor for a letter of recommendation. Of course, we accept such a transfer only if you otherwise qualify. If for any reason you cannot obtain such a letter, you should at least write your former church of your change of membership.

Not everyone can be a member of an Assemblies of God church. Your acceptance as a member is contingent on certain qualifications.

1. *The New Birth.* A local church is an assembly of Christian believers. Jesus said, "For where two or three are gathered together in my name, there am I in the midst of them" (Matthew 18:20). Two or more Christians united in worship and work become something more than the sum of their own attributes; they become the church of the living God. For this reason, only true Christian believers, persons who have experienced the new birth (see John 3:3), may become church members.

You prove the validity of your claim to the new birth by your testimony, both in word and deed. The congregation will ask you to attend the church for a while before applying for membership, so you will have the opportunity to prove yourself by your life.

2. *Water Baptism.* Because water baptism testifies to our identification with the body of Christ, it is expected that members of an Assemblies of God church be properly baptized by immersion in the name of the Father, Son, and Holy Spirit. If you have accepted Christ but have not been baptized, seek to obey the Lord on this matter at your very earliest opportunity.

3. *Unity of Faith and Practice.* Doctrinal agreement, at least on the fundamental concepts, is imperative. "Can two walk together, except they be agreed?" (Amos 3:3). "And they continued steadfastly in the apostles' doctrine and fellowship, and in breaking of bread, and in prayers" (Acts 2:42).

Practice and faith are inseparable. Practice is the outworking of faith. Included are the new birth as a definite personal experience of regeneration, water baptism by immersion, the Holy Spirit baptism with the initial physical evidence of speaking in other tongues, separation from the sins of the world, and the whole sphere of Christian activity and conduct. As an applicant, you must have followed the Lord in each of these important areas, or at least have given evidence of complete willingness to do so.

4. *Agreement in Purpose.* One of the main purposes of membership is to join yourself with a group of people with whom you basically agree. The Assemblies of God exists to worship God, provide fellowship for its members, and to make possible a united front for world evangelization.

5. *Willingness to Submit to Group Decisions and Authority.* The principle of submission is vital to spiritual life. You can never rule if you will not be ruled. As a church member, you must recognize divinely appointed leadership and be submissive to it. "Obey them that have the rule over you, and submit yourselves: for they watch for your souls, as they that must give account, that they may do it with joy, and not with grief: for that is unprofitable for you" (Hebrews 13:17).

6. *Willingness to Support the Church and Its Ministries.* One of your reasons for joining an organization is that you agree with its purposes and goals. It only stands to reason that you would support the work of such an organization with your own efforts and financial support. If you are going to share in the benefits of the church, then share in the responsibilities as well.

The sense of belonging made possible through church membership is a valuable asset to any Christian, for it is somewhat akin to being a member of a family. Sad is the state of the person who has no place to call home; and sad is the condition of the Christian who does not belong to a church family where he can enjoy all the privileges of the fellowship and the delights of sharing the responsibilities.

It is within this context of lasting human relationships that a church can attain its highest degree of worship to God. The Lord dearly loves a church that demonstrates continuity and longevity.

Christians are strengthened and established in an environment of responsible membership. Freelance Christians, who shun membership so they may wander where they choose, deprive themselves of the very thing that can do them the most good. They lack stability, and so fail to mature normally. Furthermore, they do not participate meaningfully in worship, fellowship, or evangelism.

The sense of belonging is as important to children as to adults. The parent who does not provide his child with a stable, responsible home church is depriving him of a vital facet of life and doing him irreparable damage (see Proverbs 22:6).

Purity of Christian life is another result of this sense of belonging. Through its disciplining and teaching role, the church guides the lives of its members into wholesome and godly behavior. Our Lord used the threat of lost membership in the household of God to correct the church at Sardis. "Thou hast a few names even in Sardis which have not defiled their garments; and they shall walk with me in white:

for they are worthy. He that overcometh, the same shall be clothed in white raiment; and I will not blot out his name out of the book of life" (Revelation 3:4,5).

Through church membership the church is supported and is able to carry out its task of ministry to God through worship, ministry to the saints through fellowship, and ministry to the lost through evangelism. "And all that believed were together, and had all things common. . . . And the Lord added to the church daily such as should be saved" (Acts 2:44,47).

Church membership certainly cannot save anyone; but it does help provide a society of the saved, a fellowship of the redeemed, a foretaste of the kingdom of God's people whose names are written in the Book of Life.

King David offered excellent advice—"Let the redeemed of the Lord say so" (Psalm 107:2). If you have been saved by the blood of Christ, declare yourself and join yourself to a responsible home church.

10 King of Your Life

While crossing the Irish Channel one dark, starless night, F. B. Meyer stood on the deck by the captain and asked, "How do you know Holyhead Harbor on such a dark night as this?"

The captain replied, "You see those three lights? Those three must line up behind each other as one, and when we see them so united we know the exact position of the harbor's mouth."

Impressed by the simplicity of the guidance system, F. B. Meyer later wrote, "When we want to know God's will there are three things which always concur—the inward impulse, the Word of God, and the trend of circumstances! God in the heart, impelling us forward. God in His Book, corroborating whatever He says in the heart; and God in circumstances, which are always indicative of His will. Never start until these three things agree."

Of all the creatures on earth, the most unusual is man. Although scientists may seek to classify him among the animals, in many ways he does not qualify for such a description. He is far more intelligent than any other creature on earth, and he is almost totally lacking in natural instincts. He begins his life with an unprogrammed mind, as if it were a clean slate, and all he does or becomes is by acting, reacting, and learning. Thus, each human being creates his own set of behavorial patterns and makes his own interpretation of the world. People are not all cast in the same mold, but are individually different one from another.

As a member of the human race, you are influenced by many things—environment, family, society, and your own internal struggle to survive and make sense of the world. Yet, your response is truly your own. You are a real person, responsible for your own decisions, acts, and attitudes; and you are capable of directing your own earthly destiny. For these reasons, you are capable of great achievements and of great conflicts.

You Are Not Alone

If you were creation's only form of intelligence, this would be a disappointing universe. The fact is you are not alone. You share your existence with other intelligent minds, some of which are of an order unlimited by physical matter. That order is the realm of spirit—ultimately the real world because God, who is Spirit, created matter and exists outside His creation. We cannot limit God to a human definition; but along with whatever else He is, He is intelligent Mind. God expresses His will both in His general creation and in the individual lives of men.

The devil also, in addition to whatever else he is, is a cunning mind that seeks to influence your life for his nefarious purposes.

You find yourself, then, in a complicated three-way struggle. Your own intelligence and ability to make free choices come into essential conflict with the will of God and the will of Satan. Three separate minds all vie for the control of your life and destiny.

Your human will seeks basically to survive on this

difficult planet either by dominating other people and situations or by following the leadership of some person or group whom you trust. God's will seeks to make you aware of His presence and your own true eternal nature and to bring your will into unity with His divine purpose for you. Satan seeks to reduce your mind to an animal plane in which you live only for the momentary satisfaction of your appetites and passions and thus blind you to your true nature.

Once you are born into the family of God, you must realize your spiritual nature and claim your eternal inheritance by bringing your human will into proper relationship with the will of God your Father. Although He has given you the power of free choice, He knows you will not have time in your short life on earth to learn to make all the right decisions. If you will surrender your will back to Him and accept His guidance through the maze of life, you will resist the will of the devil and arrive safely to your proper destiny in heaven.

Jesus came to show you how to serve the will of God; but before this can be done a foe must be defeated. This is the self-life, the flesh, which is diametrically opposed to the will of God, represented by the Cross (see Matthew 16:24).

Christian living at its very highest and best is that which is governed by complete dedication to the will of God.

KING OF YOUR LIFE

The doing of God's will is at the very heart of the Christian life. Even Jesus faced the crisis of choice between his human will and God's eternal plan when He prayed in the Garden of Gethsemane, "not my will, but thine, be done" (Luke 22:42). The apostle

Paul called himself Christ's *slave* (translated *servant* in the King James Version)—"Paul, a servant of Jesus Christ" (Romans 1:1).

The plain fact is that if you do not surrender to God's will, you probably will not inherit eternal life. Jesus said, "Not every one that saith unto me, Lord, Lord, shall enter into the kingdom of heaven; but he that doeth the will of my Father which is in heaven" (Matthew 7:21).

A key to this serious pronouncement is the word "kingdom." Where there is a kingdom there must be a king. You cannot enter the kingdom of heaven if you will not submit yourself to the King. Where is this marvelous kingdom? It is any place where God reigns. That is why Jesus could say, "The kingdom of God is within you" (Luke 17:21).

So important was God's will to Jesus that He often spoke about it. When His disciples were concerned about food, He said, "My meat is to do the will of him that sent me, and to finish his work" (John 4:34). To the multitude He said, "For I came down from heaven, not to do mine own will, but the will of him that sent me" (John 6:38).

Through the death and resurrection of Christ, God has forgiven your sins and set you upon a new course. Now, to arrive safely at your heavenly destination you must submit to His guidance and do His will.

How to Know His Will

Since the will of God is so important and since God desires that His children know and do His will (see Ephesians 5:17), it follows that God must have ways and means of making His will known (see Acts 22:14).

1. *The will of God is revealed in His Word.* Every

other supposed revelation must be able to stand up under the blazing searchlight of the Word, or it is to be rejected. The Word is the principal source for understanding God's will in all matters related to Christian life and conduct (see Psalm 119:105; 2 Peter 1:19-21).

2. *The will of God is made known by circumstances.* God does not change His will, but sometimes He must use circumstances to bring it about.

The first Christians knew that the will of God was "Go ye into all the world, and preach the gospel to every creature" (Mark 16:15), but they did not seem to want to leave the city of Jerusalem. Then came persecution (Acts 8:1), and they were scattered abroad. God used the circumstances of Jewish opposition to get His will accomplished. "Therefore they that were scattered abroad went everywhere preaching the word" (Acts 8:4).

Circumstances are God's levers with which He pries us into His will. As a Christian, you should keep an alert eye on your circumstances in an effort to fully please the Lord (see Philippians 2:13).

3. *The will of God is made known by peace in the heart.* The peace of God is the Christian's peculiar treasure. It is a sort of barometer for the soul, indicating your spiritual highs and lows. To recognize successfully God's will, you must develop a spiritual sensitivity to what He wants you to do and to what most pleases Him. If moving in a certain direction disturbs your inner peace, it may be an indication the will of God is being missed. Or, it may be that your will is conflicting with God's design.

The apostle Paul had the answer: "And let the peace of God rule in your hearts" (Colossians 3:15).

4. *The will of God is revealed by spiritual revelation.* Jesus said of the Holy Spirit, "He will guide you into all truth" (John 16:13). In this capacity He may bring you the knowledge of God's will by spiritual revelation (see Acts 8:26,27; 9:10,11; 10:9-22). He has spoken through visions or angelic visitations, and sometimes does so by activating human intuition or by dreams.

A word of warning must be sounded, however, for you can easily be misguided by revelations that originate with Satan or in your own imagination. Flatly reject any such revelation that would in any way lead you contrarily to the Word of God (see Isaiah 8:20). Whenever in doubt, let the Bible be your authoritative source.

5. *The will of God is always redemptive.* When in doubt about a certain matter or action, ask if it is in the interest of your soul's well-being and the up-building of the Kingdom. God's will is always redemptive, while that of Satan is destructive (see John 10:10).

How to Do His Will

The ideal condition exists not when your own will is subjugated, but when your will becomes the same as that of God. If your will opposes God, then it must be put down; but if it complements and unifies with the purpose of God it produces a wonderful sense of freedom and full human potentiality. God does not want unthinking robots; He wants obedient sons.

The putting down of self is a beginning phase of the Christian life. Once you have become one with God and His purpose, you enter a deeper level of being in which you develop toward your full potential self. The most perfect form of being is that of complete unity with God in which you abide in Him and He abides in you. Jesus said, "If a man love me, he will keep my words: and my Father will love him, and we will come unto him, and make our abode with him" (John 14:23).

God desires more than a willingness to do His will; He demands performance. For this reason, Paul wrote to the Corinthians, "Now therefore perform the doing of it; that as there was a readiness to will, so there may be a performance also out of that which ye have. For if there be first a willing mind, it is accepted according to that a man hath, and not according to that he hath not" (2 Corinthians 8:11,12).

Perhaps no one is better qualified to give instructions to the beginner than Mary, the mother of Jesus, for she discovered the delights of faithful submission to God's will. Her simple instruction to the servants at the wedding in Cana are still adequate for all: "Whatsoever he saith unto you, do it" (John 2:5).

A Standing Order

To all Christians of every place and time throughout the church age, God has given us His standing order: "Go ye into all the world, and preach the gospel to every creature" (Mark 16:15).

Whatever else you do in obedience to God's will, you must somehow relate meaningfully to this basic commission. Either you must go and preach or you must stay and send. The task must be done either by you or by those whom you assist in the fulfillment of God's command. For this you need no special revelation or individual calling (although God may speak to you about it or call you to some specific duty); it is a basic marching order to God's army.

God called a missionary to a foreign land, and on one occasion the missionary laid his hand on the forehead of a lame man and prayed for his healing. The man was instantly healed, and he exclaimed, "God touched me!"

"But it was the missionary who touched you," someone objected.

"Ah," said the healed man, "but he touched me for God."

Yes, that is the secret—to become so much at one with God that you act on His behalf! It is this complete submission to His will that God seeks in His children.

If God is king of your life, then you are His subject and are amenable to His will. An old hymn says, "trust and obey, for there's no other way, to be happy in Jesus, but to trust and obey." To trust is to believe, and to obey is to surrender your will. In these two actions and attitudes are the essence of the Christian life and the key to effective Christian service.

11 A Vision for the Lost

India contains more than 750,000 villages, many of which never have been visited by a missionary. So numerous are these villages that if Jesus Christ had remained on earth and had visited a different Indian village each day for all these years, there still would be thousands of villages for Him to visit!

When we consider the great population of unevangelized people on earth, it seems almost impossible to take the gospel of Christ to every place and every person. Yet, Jesus died for all people and He expects His church to tell everyone the good news. It is possible to reach all the lost with the message of Christ, but it will take the vision and dedication of all Christians to accomplish the Great Commission "Go ye into all the world, and preach the gospel to every creature" (Mark 16:15).

Vision is of first importance to the Christian mission. In fact, it is perhaps the most vital element in church life, for upon it hangs not only the salvation of lost men, but the spiritual well-being of saved men. Where there is no vision, no lost will be saved, and the church itself will suffer irreparable loss (see Proverbs 29:18).

THE SOURCE OF VISION

One of the problems of human perception is the

difference between what really exists and what we think we see.

Jesus experienced no difficulty of vision for the lost, for He knew the true state of man and addressed himself to the need realistically. The Bible says, "He knew what was in man" (John 2:25).

For you as a Christian, the task of seeing the true state of the lost may be somewhat more difficult, for once you leave the ways of sin and live within the protective atmosphere of the church and the grace of God you may easily forget what it was like to live outside of God's light.

What if no one had told you about Jesus Christ and His love? What if you had been born in a country where not one person in your whole village had ever heard the story of Jesus? You would be lost. And if no one ever became concerned about your condition, you would be lost forever.

Where may you get the vision necessary to win lost men and women to Christ? Surely a mere theological concept of man's lost condition will not adequately serve the purpose. Only a clear, unobstructed, realistic vision will do.

Vision is a result of a deliberate act of looking. This is true both naturally and spiritually.

The story is told of a man who one day complimented his wife on her new dress, only to learn she had been wearing the garment for two years. He just had not noticed it. Likewise, the lost are everywhere about us, but we do not see them as such. We see them living next door or across the street. We rub shoulders with them at work. We move among them every day. If we are not captivated by a vision of their true state, they will remain lost.

Jesus gave us the key to the necessary vision. "Say not ye, There are yet four months, and then cometh harvest? behold, I say unto you, Lift up your eyes, and look on the fields; for they are white already to harvest" (John 4:35).

His meaning is clear: We are not to procrastinate in our evangelistic action, but are to give our full attention to the world's harvest of souls.

Solomon said, "Where there is no vision, the people perish" (Proverbs 29:18). The ancient king could not have known what his words would mean for us; yet they ring true. Both the saved and the lost suffer if the church does not open its eyes and look at its true task in the world.

ARE THE UNSAVED REALLY LOST?

Not all who are lost are aware of their condition. Some travel the broad road of sin unknowingly, unmindful of the end because the path of life has not been pointed out to them. Others have chosen the broad road and travel it purposely, loving darkness rather than light. They have shunned the strait gate and narrow way because it is too restrictive for them (see Matthew 7:13,14).

But whether men travel this way because they do not know or because they will not hear, it still "leadeth to destruction, and many there be which go in thereat" (v. 13). Until the Christian sees that men are really lost, he will very likely do little to see them saved.

Recent studies of world population indicate that at least half the people of the world have yet to receive an adequate Christian witness. However, as staggering as statistical evidence may be concerning the multitudes of unchurched and unsaved people, such studies generally fall short of moving Christians to meaningful action. Only a divinely imparted awareness of the awful fact of man's lostness and eternal damnation can produce the necessary motivation.

Some have the idea that Jesus was moved with compassion merely by seeing the multitudes, but such was not the case. Matthew 9:36 says, "But when he saw the multitudes, he was moved with compassion on them, because they fainted, and were scattered abroad, as sheep having no shepherd." What moved Him was the same thing that will move us. He saw beyond the surface and perceived of the multitude as lost souls in desperate need; they were weak, scattered, and lost.

Consider the chain of evidence of the fact that men are lost:

1. "All we like sheep have gone astray; we have turned every one to his own way" (Isaiah 53:6).

2. "Broad is the way, that leadeth to destruction" (Matthew 7:13).

3. "For the Son of man is come to seek and to save that which was lost" (Luke 19:10).

4. "For we have before proved both Jews and Gentiles, that they are all under sin; as it is written, There is none righteous, no, not one: there is none that understandeth, there is none that seeketh after God. They are all gone out of the way, they are together become unprofitable; there is none that doeth good, no, not one" (Romans 3:9-12).

5. "Wherefore, as by one man sin entered into the world, and death by sin; and so death passed upon all men, for that all have sinned" (Romans 5:12).

6. "We thus judge, that if one died for all, then were all dead" (2 Corinthians 5:14).

There are only two kinds of people in the world,

the lost and the saved. The lost are lost because they are like sheep without a shepherd. They are without orientation, because they can see only their immediate material world. The saved are saved because they are former lost who have found their Shepherd and know where they are and where they are going.

The lost will perish in their sins; but the saved will live forever in the presence of God. "For God so loved the world, that he gave his only begotten Son, that whosoever believeth in him should not perish, but have everlasting life. For God sent not his Son into the world to condemn the world; but that the world through him might be saved" (John 3:16,17).

THE STATE OF THE LOST

One of the most graphic descriptions of the lost is in Ephesians 2:1-3—"And you hath he quickened, who were dead in trespasses and sins; wherein in time past ye walked according to the course of this world, according to the prince of the power of the air, the spirit that now worketh in the children of disobedience: among whom also we all had our conversation in times past in the lusts of our flesh, fulfilling the desires of the flesh and of the mind; and were by nature the children of wrath, even as others."

The lost suffer both in life and in death. Even in life they are really dead, for spiritual death is the most profound death of all.

Adam and Eve were warned that in the day they ate of the forbidden fruit they would surely die. Although they disobeyed God and ate the fruit, they did not die physically that day. It is true that death set in and began its ghastly work; but in the very day when they sinned Adam and Eve died spiritually— that is, they were separated from God.

The New Testament also refers to the lost as being dead. "Many be dead" (Romans 5:15). "Who were dead in trespasses and sins" (Colossians 2:13). "But she that liveth in pleasure is dead while she liveth" (1 Timothy 5:6).

The Bible also says the lost are blind to spiritual truth. "They be blind leaders of the blind" (Matthew 15:14). "In whom the god of this world hath blinded the minds of them that believe not" (2 Corinthians 4:4). Therein is the awful truth of the state of the lost: The devil has blinded their minds. There is no darkness so deep as that of sin. We who have come unto the light of truth should be very grateful. "That ye should show forth the praises of him who hath called you out of darkness" (1 Peter 2:9).

The state of the lost in death is perhaps best portrayed in the account of the rich man and Lazarus, recorded in Luke 16:19-31. Note the following facts about the rich man's condition after death:

1. He was conscious (v. 23).

2. He had the use of his senses (v. 24).

3. He was tormented (v. 25).

4. He was separated from the righteous (v. 26).

5. He was concerned that his family be warned against the awful place in which he found himself (vv. 27,28).

Spiritual death is separation from God, not loss of consciousness. Those who fail to accept the life of God in Christ must face the awful realization that in living for the world they have forfeited their claim to heaven.

THE END OF THE LOST

Although the Bible gives us an outline of the future, we can but dimly understand the final end of the lost. Revelation 20:13-15 says, "And the sea gave up the dead which were in it; and death and hell delivered up the dead which were in them: and they were judged every man according to their works. And death and hell were cast into the lake of fire. This is the second death. And whosoever was not found written in the book of life was cast into the lake of fire."

The destiny of the wicked is eternal separation from God and that eternal suffering of His wrath known as the second death.

There is a certain teaching called universalism, which attempts to prove that all men will eventually be saved; but the serious student of the Scriptures must believe in the truth of Jesus' statement—"I am the way, the truth, and the life: no man cometh unto the Father, but by me" (John 14:6). No man can be saved by his ignorance or rejection of the truth, but must approach God only through Jesus Christ.

The word *hell* is used quite unspecifically in the Scriptures. At times it refers only to the grave. Elsewhere, it means the state of the wicked dead before the final judgment. Yet again it seems to indicate the eternal condition in the lake of fire called the second death.

Hell is described as a place of extreme suffering (Revelation 20:10), memory and remorse (Luke 16: 19-31), unsatisfied desire (Luke 16:24), contempt (Daniel 12:2), vile companionship (Revelation 21: 8), and hopelessness (Proverbs 11:7; Matthew 25:41).

The responsibility of the Christian is well stated in the book *Personal Worker's Course*:

It may be to the savage in the hideousness of his paint and nakedness; to the merchant in the filth of an Eastern bazaar; to the temple devotee with all the vileness of his heathen practices; the sad-eyed Latin-American kneeling before a wayside crucifix, worshiping at the feet of a dead Christ whom he cannot know; or it may be the man at the desk in the office, the man at the machine in the shop, the one from whom the meat is bought, the pupil in the Sunday school class, the neighbor just beyond the fence, the brother, the father. It matters not who it may be, or where; the soul that is lost is our responsibility and our opportunity.

A father had taught his children that whenever the family would be involved in a large crowd they should make some previous agreement for a meeting place, so that any member who might become lost could return to that predetermined spot and be found.

God our Father has given us such a point of discovery where we can orient ourselves and be saved from our lostness. That place is the cross of Jesus Christ. The Cross stands high above the horizon of human life and signals to all that every man can be saved from his lost condition and brought back into the care of his Heavenly Father.

12 A Heart for the Harvest

A Washington State farmer wept as he watched the rain falling on his freshly mowed alfalfa crop. His immobile baler sat dripping in the field, and the men who were going to help him just gazed expressionlessly at the drenching rain. After so many months of waiting, the harvest was lost.

The farmer's sorrow was caused by more than the loss of the winter's hay. For days before the coming of the rain the sun had shone brightly in the sky and the hay had been ready to mow. But the farmer had put off the harvest because he was so busy with other things. He thought the sun would continue to shine and the harvest would wait for his convenience. Now, he sat and wept with remorse at his own misjudgment.

An old saying goes: "Time and tide wait for no man." The harvest doesn't wait, either. When the harvest is ready, the workers must bring it in or lose it forever. And they must put their hearts into their work, for once the harvest is ripe the harvesting is critical.

Jesus chose fishermen and tax collectors for His disciples, but much of His preaching was directed to a nation of farmers. His hearers understood Him very well when He said, "The harvest truly is plenteous, but the laborers are few; pray ye therefore the Lord of the harvest, that he will send forth laborers into his harvest" (Matthew 9:37,38).

The harvest of which Jesus spoke was that of the multitudes of people for whom He had great compassion. In essence, He said, "There are a great many people in the world and too few workers to reach them all with the gospel message. Pray that God will send out more Christian workers into the harvest fields of the world."

A strange thing happens when you pray that prayer. The request to God that He send more workers into His fields almost always results in a personal challenge to the one who prays. As with Isaiah (see Isaiah 6:1-9), the question, "Whom shall I send, and who will go for us?" should lead us to the reply, "Here am I; send me." As a result, God says, "Go, and tell this people."

THE NEED FOR HARVESTERS

There is nothing quite so tragic as a harvest that goes unreaped. The harvest is the fruit of labor expended, and to see it fall to the ground is a most disturbing experience. It disturbs our Lord. By His own travail and labor He has brought about the possibility of an abundant harvest of souls. He said, "Lift up your eyes, and look on the fields; for they are white already to harvest" (John 4:35).

The Lord has commanded His workers to bring the harvest into His shelter, but the principle He taught us in the first century still applies today: There are not enough laborers for the size of the task. For that reason, every Christian believer must relate in some

111

meaningful way to the task of total world evangelization.

There is a twofold need: (1) souls are in need of the Lord, and (2) the Lord is in need of laborers.

Before you can have compassion toward lost men and successfully pursue their souls, you must recognize human need. Compassion cannot exist where there is no need, for it is basically a willingness and compulsion to involve yourself deeply and lovingly in other people's problems. The capacity for compassion is innate in every Christian; but it only manifests itself in response to human need. To develop and maintain compassion for the lost you must be aware of the true condition of the lost and direct your efforts toward local and world evangelization.

Compassion unexpressed dies, but compassion expressed grows (see Matthew 18:33). If you can see the great masses of men as lost and doomed to God's wrath unless they accept the gospel of Christ, you will do all in your power to save them from their awful fate.

Hurricane winds were building along the Gulf Coast, and the residents of a small town closed their shutters and doors against the force of the storm. Each family closed itself within its own house to wait out the tempest. But then came the call, "A child is missing in the streets!" Men who had planned to hide from the storm then put on their wraps and went out into the face of the winds and rain until they had found the lost child and brought him into the safety of his father's house. What made the difference? It was compassion for a lost child. That is the same force that will drive us out of our complacency and personal comfort to bring a world of lost children into their Father's house.

Yes, the world has a great need. And, the Lord has a need, too. He needs you. His whole plan of caring for the needs of the world revolves around the response and involvement of His people. He said, "As my Father hath sent me, even so send I you" (John 20:21).

THE GREAT COMMISSION

The divinely appointed task of the church is clear, for our Lord said, "Go ye therefore, and teach all nations, baptizing them in the name of the Father, and of the Son, and of the Holy Ghost: teaching them to observe all things whatsoever I have commanded you: and lo, I am with you alway, even unto the end of the world. Amen" (Matthew 28:19,20).

The threefold mission of the church is to minister to God in worship, to the saints in teaching and fellowship, and to the world in evangelism. Although the Great Commission sends us to fulfill the latter of these three functions, when we properly evangelize the world we produce more churches in our own land and around the world. The churches we establish elsewhere also take up the tasks and blessings of worship, teaching, fellowship, and evangelism, so that the chain of Christian service continues.

You must perform your task at two levels. First, you must involve yourself in personal witness to the lost. This means basically that you must use your personal contacts with people as opportunities to proclaim the gospel—that central core of Christian truth concerned with the death and resurrection of Jesus Christ and their implication on individual human lives. Second, you must involve yourself with the broad scope of group ministries through your church.

Through individual and group witnessing, the church is responsible to God to spread the knowledge of Jesus Christ and His message to every man, woman, and child on the face of the earth. Although personal evangelism is very effective for making Christian converts, the world is too large and the population too great for the task to be finished in this generation by individual efforts alone. The churches must band together in a missionary strategy and approach the Great Commission with serious intentions of making a dedicated effort if we are to accomplish what God has commanded.

There should be no conflict of interests between local church activities, the evangelization of our own country, and our mission to the rest of the world. To anyone who would carry out one part of the church's task at the expense of the rest, the words of Jesus apply: "These ought ye to have done, and not to leave the other undone" (Matthew 23:23). There are enough resources and recruits in the existing churches to carry out our whole task in this generation, if our people will only dedicate themselves to the fulfillment of the Great Commission and be wise enough to select effective methods to accomplish their goals.

AMBASSADORS FOR CHRIST

When you became a Christian, you also became a citizen of heaven who is living temporarily in an alien land. Your purpose here on earth is to act on behalf of your King and deliver His messages to the people. The King of kings and Lord of lords has greatly honored you by naming you His own ambassador.

The Bible puts it this way: "And all things are of God, who hath reconciled us to himself by Jesus Christ, and hath given to us the ministry of reconciliation; to wit, that God was in Christ, reconciling the world unto himself, not imputing their trespasses unto them; and hath committed unto us the word of reconciliation. Now then we are ambassadors for Christ" (2 Corinthians 5:18-20).

What a high privilege it is to be an ambassador for Christ and act in His stead on behalf of lost men. Indeed, you are an ambassador with portfolio, for your assignment is clear. Men and God have become separated, and you are to reconcile them through the message that God was in Christ to provide forgiveness of sin and the reestablishing of fellowship. The ministry of every ambassador for Christ is to alert sinful men to what Christ has done for them and to help establish congregations of Christian believers in every community on the face of the earth.

How to Be a Witness

The ways and means of seeking the lost are many and varied, but there are some basic approaches to the matter that will help you find your most effective Christian ministry.

1. *Be filled With the Spirit.* Jesus said, "But ye shall receive power, after that the Holy Ghost is come upon you: and ye shall be witnesses unto me both in Jerusalem, and in all Judea, and in Samaria, and unto the uttermost part of the earth" (Acts 1:8).

The early Christians had phenomenal success in their pursuit of the lost; but this was not without reason. At the very outset they joined forces with the Holy Spirit in the holy occupation of seeking the lost. They could not have done it alone, but with the supernatural power of the Holy Spirit and the intensification of their own powers by divine inspiration they boldly spoke the Word and testified before all men.

The Lord knows your limitations better than you do, but He also knows that if He fills you with His Holy Spirit you can do anything, speak to anyone, or go to any place on His mission.

2. *Deliver His Message.* No method is more effective in bringing lost men to Christ than the right message. Almost without exception the conversions recorded in the New Testament can be traced to a specific message that reached the hearts of unsaved men.

The early Christians were totally dedicated to this message. The occasion mattered not; the message had to be delivered, whether to the multitude on the Day of Pentecost (Acts 2:22-24), to the crowd at the Beautiful Gate after the lame man's healing (Acts 3:13-15), to the Sanhedrin when it demanded an explanation for a miracle (Acts 4:8-12), to a lonely individual on a desert road (Acts 8:27-39), or to the Jews in a synagogue (Acts 17:1-3).

What was the message? Was it some truth so profound that only the learned could understand and proclaim it? No! That message was the gospel, that central core of Christian truth about the death and resurrection of Jesus Christ. Paul wrote: "Moreover, brethren, I declare unto you the gospel which I preached unto you, which also ye have received, and wherein ye stand; by which also ye are saved. . . . For I delivered unto you first of all that which I also received, how that Christ died for our sins according to the Scriptures; and that he was buried, and that he rose again the third day according to the Scriptures" (1 Corinthians 15:1-4).

This is the message, the gospel of Christ. It is so simple that any Christian can proclaim it; and yet it is so powerful that it can transform any sinner into a saint. The body of Christian truth is vastly profound, but the proclamation of its central message is utterly simple. The gospel was the message of the first Christians, and it must be ours today.

3. *Support the Proclamation of the Gospel.* As a Christian, you really have no choice in whether to become involved in evangelism. It is your Christian nature and your commandment to proclaim the gospel. You either must proclaim the gospel to every man, woman, and child on earth, or else you must join your efforts to those of other Christians to make world evangelization possible. You should do both—witness to all people with whom you come into personal contact, and join with others to send missionaries out to the world.

The Lord never intended that everyone should become a preacher, or else there would be no one sitting in the pew or supporting the work of the church.

Make it your practice to give regularly to your church's missionary program, for only by united and purposeful action can we evangelize our world. How much should you give? The question is not so much the amount you give as it is what you have left. Most missions-minded Christians give tithes and offerings for the support of their local churches and then give their missionary offerings in addition. There are many appeals through the mail and over radio and television, but the best way to make the wisest use of your missionary offering is to give it through your church, designated for general missions or a specific missionary or project.

4. *Take Advantage of Your Opportunities.* The Holy Spirit is constantly working to bring men to Christ, and He needs to be able to use any child of God at any time to talk to anybody. He most often uses the plan of bringing people across your path and expecting you to take advantage of the opportunity. This is a great blessing and a tremendous responsibility.

5. *Listen for His Call to Christian Service.* The Lord may want you to accept certain responsibilities in your local church, or He might ask you to enter a career of Christian ministry. He calls some believers to be teachers, pastors, or missionaries. Do not fear His call, but glady and humbly accept any assignment He may give you.

In most cases, those who are called to a career of Christian ministry should attend a Bible college and prepare themselves well, for the demands on today's ministry are great.

A Missionary Commitment

Since its very beginning in 1914, the Assemblies of God has been an intensely missionary church. All its people—pastors, missionaries, leaders, and laymen—have dedicated themselves to total world evangelization to such a degree that it has become the fastest growing evangelical church in the world. In the United States the Assemblies of God is developing very rapidly, and in foreign missionary lands it doubles its numbers of believers every seven years.

The founders wrote in their official minutes of 1914, "We pledge ourselves and the Movement to

Him for the greatest evangelism that the world has ever seen."

You have become a part of a dedicated family of people who take the Great Commission of Christ seriously and work with great fervor for its fulfillment.

13 What's in a Name?

"Why," asked a sincere inquirer, "must there be different church groups? Why can't they all get together in one great church?"

"There are two reasons," a pastor replied. "First, if such a huge single organization would get into the wrong hands it could compromise too much with the world and lose its apostolic Christian character. The second reason is that life doesn't work that way."

"What do you mean?" asked the inquirer.

The pastor responded, "Wherever there is life there is diversification of life forms. Notice all the different leaves and grasses and birds and animals that fill the whole environment with a balanced ecology? It is only in deterioration and decay that life forms become unified into a similar mass. In human activities there is always a difference of opinion and diversification of emphasis as long as an issue is alive and thriving. Unification and compromise are signs of decay."

The inquirer seemed surprised. "You mean that the many kinds of churches are a good sign?"

"Exactly," the pastor replied. "Christianity is alive and growing, and so it diversifies to reach all kinds of people and emphasize all of Christ's teachings. The idea of one large ecumenical church would destroy true apostolic Christianity."

It is very important that you understand and appreciate the particular branch of Christianity of which you have become a part.

The Pentecostal Movement is that body of Christian believers who seek a full return to the doctrines, the religious experiences, the practices, and the priorities of the first-century, Apostolic Church.

The Assemblies of God, which is our particular fellowship within this Movement, is the largest and most widespread in the world of all the Pentecostal churches. It is evangelical and Pentecostal in doctrine, congregational in government, missionary in spirit, and generally informal in style. Although it teaches a fully developed Christian theology based on apostolic standards (see Chapter 8), it emphasizes four important concepts that affect individual human experience: (1) salvation through the blood of Christ, (2) the baptism in the Holy Spirit, (3) divine healing and other miraculous answers to prayer, and (4) the second coming of Christ.

The Pentecostal position results from a specific view of church history. In the beginning of the Christian faith the church was characterized by certain doctrines, experiences, practices, and priorities. Its doctrines were the teachings of Christ, its experiences were personal and miraculous, its practices were practical and direct, and its priorities were on personal piety and evangelistic action.

Over the following centuries the church lost its original character and concepts. It mixed too much with pagan thoughts and practices, and the people became separated from their apostolic source in the New Testament Scriptures. The Bible was lost to the common people, buried in liturgical use, and unknown except in the dying Latin language. The Christian faith became diluted with paganism beyond recognition.

With the invention of the printing press and the translation of the Bible into contemporary languages, the New Testament was restored to the common people. The Reformation was inevitable once men asked the question—"Why isn't our church like the Apostolic Church?"

Step by step since the Reformation of the 15th century, the church has been moving back to apostolic Christianity. Martin Luther stressed justification by faith and a belief in the Bible as the infallible Word of God. John and Charles Wesley stressed salvation as a personal experience and evangelism as the church's divinely appointed task. Subsequent revival movements emphasized the faith of the common man and the importance of prayer and Bible study. By the late 19th century there were a great many Bible conferences, and most Bible-based churches operated active Sunday schools for children and adults. With the emphasis on the Word of God, the increasing availability of Bibles, and the growth of literacy and education among the popular masses, it was only a matter of time before some Bible readers would insist on a full return to New Testament Christianity with its doctrines, religious experiences, practices, and priorities. Thus, at the turn of the 20th century, was born the Pentecostal Movement.

A Pentecostal Christian identifies himself with the birth of the Apostolic Church on the Day of Pentecost in A.D. 30. He sees himself as an apostolic believer and his church as a rebirth of apostolic Christianity. Although he believes in the evangelization of the popular masses, he does not sacrifice his intellect on the altar of practical expediency. He believes his theology is sound, his methods are successful, and his faith is satisfying. While he places great importance on personal experience in religion and at times may be noted for his emotional response in worship, he has established more Bible schools around the world for the intellectual and practical training of ministers than has any other Christian group.

An emotionally responsive, intellectually active Christian with a strongly developed sense of evangelistic responsibility, the Pentecostal has changed the character of 20th-century Christianity and poses a threat to lesser activated forms of the church and to the non-Christian world. He fully intends to convince the whole world of his faith and conviction; and his record to date indicates he may very well do exactly what he has proposed.

In spite of his apparent forcefulness and zeal, he is not an egocentric person. In love with Jesus Christ and empowered by the Holy Spirit, he sees himself as a messenger of God's love and salvation and interprets his own response in terms of personal holiness and evangelistic action. He believes that Jesus Christ will return to earth, very likely within this century; and he dedicates himself to the rapid evangelization of the world.

THE ASSEMBLIES OF GOD

At first, the existing churches did not know what to do with the new Pentecostals. Many churches said they were of the devil and expelled them from their own membership. Pentecostal believers then formed their own churches and began to make converts directly into what they called full-gospel congregations.

In April, 1914, Pentecostal ministers and laymen from around the country met at Hot Springs, Arkansas to form the Assemblies of God. The opening statement of their official minutes was: "For a number of years, God has been leading men to seek for a full apostolic gospel standard of experience and doctrine."

Two Pentecostal magazines helped unite the Assemblies of God—the *Word and Witness,* edited by E. H. Bell, and the *Christian Evangel,* edited by J. Roswell Flower. Bell became the chairman of the Hot Springs meeting, and Flower was the secretary. After the founding of the Gospel Publishing House, first at St. Louis and later (1918) in Springfield, Missouri, the *Christian Evangel* became the *Weekly Evangel* and shortly thereafter *The Pentecostal Evangel.*

The founding fathers were impelled by clear-cut objectives: (1) to attain better understanding and doctrinal harmony, (2) to study ways and means of evangelizing the world and conserving the results of their labors, (3) to discuss the handling of missionary funds, (4) to investigate the possibilities of chartering churches, and (5) to evaluate the possibilities of establishing a Bible school. Later that year they established their Pentecostal literature ministry.

Today, the Assemblies of God is the fastest growing church in the world. The simplicity of its doctrinal position has been a source of great harmony. Its practical and strongly motivated method of evangelization has led to phenomenal worldwide growth. Its home and foreign missionary programs have effectively gained the financial support of its people and have produced very well at a minimum of administrative overhead. Its organization has allowed pastors and congregations to work together for common goals and discipline, while still retaining a high degree of local self-government. Its Bible schools are actively training ministers and other gospel workers all over the world. And, its literature programs provide many tons of gospel literature daily for its rapidly growing constituency.

Our Church Organization

Each local assembly has the right of self-government. It acquires and holds its own properties and elects its own pastor and church board. It transacts its own business and disciplines its own members within the general guidelines of the national and district organization.

All districts are organized basically on the same pattern. The district officers are the superintendent, assistant superintendent, secretary, treasurer, and other such officers as may be required. Most districts have departmental heads who supervise specific areas of work. In addition, there are sectional presbyters who together with the executive officers make up the district presbytery, which is the official board of the district.

The national organization is led by a general superintendent, assistant general superintendent, secretary, and treasurer. These plus the executive director of foreign missions and other executive presbyters from around the country, form the Executive Presbytery. An even larger body made up of representatives of all the districts is the General Presbytery. And, over all the fellowship is the General Council, which meets every two years and consists of ordained ministers and church delegates.

The international headquarters of the Assemblies of God is in Springfield, Missouri, which was chosen for its central position in the country. There are located the administrative offices and the various divisional and departmental service agencies of the church.

The basic unit of the church is the gathering of believers in a local body in the name of Jesus Christ. All else in our movement exists for the purpose of making Christian converts and gathering them in Christ-honoring, Bible-believing, Pentecostal congregations.

We see our ministry as threefold: (1) to minister to the Lord in worship and dedication, (2) to minister to the saints in fellowship and teaching, and (3) to minister to the world in evangelism and church establishing.

The Reverend Thomas F. Zimmerman, general superintendent for many years, has said, "Our objectives for the future must be the same ones that motivated the founders of the organization. Greatest of all is that of reaching the world for Christ. All other objectives must be subservient to this one. To this end we must continue to strengthen our efforts and improve our methods. We must undergird our spiritual life with prayer, with the reading of God's Word, and with an overflowing Spirit-filled life."

WHERE WE GOT OUR NAME

Shakespeare said, "What's in a name? that which we call a rose, by any other name would smell as sweet." We can't agree entirely with him, gifted bard that he may have been. The names of objects such as roses do not affect the nature of the object, but not so for names of human institutions. The name becomes a part of the thing itself and forms a part of its total image.

A successful church name must be simple and direct, descriptive of the nature of the church, and Biblically based. You would think that all such names would already have been chosen.

When E. H. Bell first printed the call for the Hot Springs meeting in the December 20, 1913, issue of *Word and Witness,* he addressed the announcement to "The Pentecostal Saints and Churches of God in Christ."

That first description of what was to become the Assemblies of God was too long and too similar to other church names. Some suggestions were Apostolic Faith, Church of God, and Church of God in Christ; but other groups had prior claims to them.

The name Assemblies of God probably can be traced to T. K. Leonard, whose ordination papers show him to have been ordained by the Christian Church in 1901, and then by "The Assemblies of God, Findlay, Ohio," April 14, 1912—two years before the first General Council.

The simplicity of "Assemblies of God" appealed to the delegates. It was simple and direct, described the nature of the church, and was taken right out of the Bible. The Greek word translated *church* in our English Bibles means literally *assembly.* So, the apostle Paul wrote to the Assembly of God at Corinth (1 Corinthians 1:2), the assemblies of Galatia (Galatians 1:2), and the assembly of the Thessalonians (1 Thessalonians 1:1).

You will sometimes see the church called The General Council of the Assemblies of God. The form of the name distinguishes the national church from the district councils. It refers specifically to the biennial conference. A local church either is an Assembly of God or an Assemblies of God church.

A FINAL WORD

The apostle Paul offers you excellent advice in his Epistle to Titus (2:11-15): "For the grace of God that bringeth salvation hath appeared to all men, teaching us that, denying ungodliness and worldly lusts, we should live soberly, righteously, and godly, in this present world; looking for that blessed hope, and the glorious appearing of the great God and our Saviour Jesus Christ; who gave himself for us, that he might redeem us from all iniquity, and purify unto himself a peculiar people, zealous of good works. These things speak, and exhort, and rebuke with all authority."

Welcome to the household of faith and to the Assemblies of God. Dedicate your whole life to Christ and join us in the total evangelization of the world.